HOW (NOT) TO CREATE A WINNING STRATEGY

FROM THE **HOW-NOT-TO GUIDES FOR LEADERS** SERIES

HOW (NOT) TO CREATE A WINNING STRATEGY

MARY E. MARSHALL & KIM OBBINK

Indigo River Publishing

How (NOT) To Create A Winning Strategy

© 2020 by Mary E. Marshall and Kim Obbink

Edited by Tanner Chau, Joshua Owens, and Regina Cornell
Cover and interior design by Robin Vuchnich
Illustrations by Robin Vuchnich

Indigo River Publishing
3 West Garden Street, Ste. 718
Pensacola, FL 32502
www.indigoriverpublishing.com

Ordering Information:

Quantity sales: Special discounts are available on quantity purchases by corporations, associations, and others. For details, contact the publisher at the address above.

Orders by US trade bookstores and wholesalers: Please contact the publisher at the address above.

Printed in the United States of America

Library of Congress Control Number: 2019957542

ISBN: 978-1-950906-42-0 (paperback), 978-1-950906-44-4 (ebook)

First Edition

*With Indigo River Publishing, you can always expect great books, strong voices, and meaningful messages. Most importantly, you'll always find...*words worth reading.

CONTENTS

SECTION 3

ABOUT THE AUTHORS

PREFACE

Ever sat through a strategic planning session that was facilitated by an inept facilitator or, worse, a CEO who wasn't sure what *strategy* was? Or even worse than that, the "strategic plan" was to drag out the old plan from the previous year, dust it off, make a few cosmetic changes, and call it good? These are all ways NOT to create a great strategy. Unfortunately, all of these are done more often than anyone will admit, and the result is always the same: companies miss the boat on creating a great strategy that people can actually get excited about.

This book will show you exactly what NOT to do. Twenty-four "strategies" that will not work, no matter how hard you click your heels together and wish to be transported back to a time when someone else was building your strategy. One of the biggest challenges to creating a great strategy is that a lot of leaders don't even know what a strategy is. They confuse it with a list of goals that need to be accomplished. Goals are good—they are even better when in service of a great strategy.

A strategy is a way to achieve something; it is a particular path you choose to go down to accomplish something that you or your organization wants to achieve. Say you want to make a cake; there are multiple ways to do it. When you decide to go forward, you will pick a certain strategy to make that cake based on any number of factors. There will be various tasks and goals associated with those factors, and if you're taking your cake to a bake sale, everyone will have used a different "strategy" to get their cake to market. Some will taste great! Some will be just okay. And some will be politely or not so politely deposited in the same bin with the doggie poo bags. Inedible and—like a bad business strategy—nasty, and if you eat it you are likely to be spending time on the porcelain throne wishing you had chosen more wisely.

Business strategies are—or should be—in service of a vision the organization has. Sometimes the bigger problem is the vision is really a mission, or strategic objectives are confused with goals (see above), and the result is a word salad that no one understands. Oh, and about $25–50K was paid to some guy to facilitate this dead-on-arrival plan. You know you have a stinker when as soon as the ink is dry on the document, everyone leaves the room, glad that two-day waste of time is over, and goes back to business as usual.

Don't do any of that. Read these twenty-four priceless vignettes of hapless leadership and strategic planning, and learn what NOT to do when creating a winning strategy. Why not? Let's be honest: your last strategic plan is still sitting on your shelf and no one remembers what's in it.

SECTION 1

LET'S START PLANNICKING

Giddy up! Let's go! Let's get the plan going. C'mon, c'mon, c'mon now! Yes, some leaders treat the annual planning session like a cattle roundup with one thing in mind: the plan. But don't expect them to give you a definition of what the plan might look like, who should be involved, or—God forbid—the vision that might be accomplished if you actually succeed. They relish the planning phase, as if it's the be-all and end-all of strategic planning—in other words, they start "plannicking."

Plannicking is a combination of planning and panicking because the leader doesn't know what he or she is doing, and guess what? It shows. *Plannicking* is getting everyone all spun up about the plan itself without ever bothering to answer the question: In service of what? It happens in about 90 percent of strategic planning sessions. Get your advisory board involved, read every business book, have nostalgia for the past, go with your gut, plan alone, and generally use every fad that relates to strategic planning you've ever heard of, and you'll have a strategic plan that's guaranteed to have the lifespan of a gnat.

In this section you will learn what NOT to do during the planning phase. As a famous leader once said, "Plans are worthless, but planning is everything." But, through inept planning, having the wrong players on the bus and in the wrong seats will guarantee that you won't accomplish a thing. You'll end up with words on paper that mean nothing, not even to you.

You can't fake the planning phase. Well, you can, but everyone knows you're faking it. Like the emperor with no clothes whom everyone compliments for being dressed in the best garments, they KNOW you're faking it. The team will dutifully carry out the plan—at least to your face—even when it's bollocks, which is a face-plant of the worst kind because it has the leader's name all over it.

So buckle up, cowgirls and cowboys, and read a little about how NOT to round up your cattle as you start the planning phase, and you just might avoid the pitfalls of so many of your fellow leaders.

CHAPTER 1

YOUR ADVISORY BORED

Sent: July 14, 10:30 a.m.
From: CEO
To: Executive Team
Subject: New Advisory Board Meeting at Noon

All,

Today at noon will be the first meeting of our new advisory board. I want each of you to be prepared to present and speak on where your department is, as it relates to the strategic plan. You will have five minutes each, so just the highlights and don't go into detail, but be prepared to answer any specifics.

The meeting is mandatory. Sorry for the short notice, but I think my assistant forgot to send out the notice last week.

BB

A great way to look like a real company is to have a board of some sort. An advisory board frees you from actually giving them any real authority, so it's definitely the way to go. The reason you would want to have this is so that when people ask, you can say you have a board, which sounds very official.

The choosing of the board members is crucial. You don't want anyone too smart or too bossy because that would undermine your leadership. Choose your friends who also want to enhance their reputations and may want something from you in the future—it's a way for them to pay it forward.

Don't bother with areas of the company that may need help and for which you might need an outside view. Go to the areas of the company that you are a real expert on. For instance, if you are a great marketer, make sure to have someone with marketing expertise on the board—although be very careful to make sure they understand YOU are the expert, not them. If you have a person who manages your buckets of cash, put them on the board as a little reward for what they do for you. You'll never have to worry about them questioning you.

The key is loyalty. If anyone you choose questions you, boot them off immediately. You want this to be a feel-good meeting that reinforces your leadership brilliance, not one that questions it. As always, show up late, leave early, or skip the meetings altogether to show that you are in charge.

Make your team prepare for the meetings, and let them think that the board actually has a say or that how each of them performs matters. The board can feel good about itself by criticizing your team members and putting them down; then you can double down on this and let them know how embarrassing their performance was. It's great to have a board to back up your opinions and keep the troops in line. This way, everything you've been saying is constantly reinforced.

Paying your board can be tricky. You could pay them for meetings; but if they'll do it for future equity, that might be a better way. Because, as you know, you'll kick them off the board before they ever get to exercise their shares. Make sure the agreement states that the shares are of no value if they no longer serve on the board. On the other hand, paying them a good rate for attending the meetings lets them know how successful and generous you are, so it could look good for you too. Keep in mind, you could use both strategies depending upon who the board member is. If it's someone you really want, pay them a lot, and if it's someone who's already a lapdog, just give them nonexistent shares. Make sure you impress upon them how "confidential" their arrangement is so they don't talk among themselves.

As for frequency of meetings, quarterly is fine as long as it fits your schedule. Make sure the entire team prepares rigorously with spreadsheets, updates, PowerPoints, and reports so that it literally consumes everyone's activity once per quarter. This makes it seem very official. But if they don't get to present or you have to change the board meeting for any reason, don't sweat it. Just tell the team they are now more prepared for next time.

Remember, a board is purely an accessory; you don't need them to augment your leadership. What they do is reinforce what you are already doing, like having a mirror on the wall that tells you what a great leader you are!

LET'S GET REAL

Having an advisory board or a true board is important for your business. But not how BB uses it. It gives you an outside perspective in those areas that are important to the growth and health of your business. Finance, acquisition, marketing, sales, systems, technology, and online and industry experience are just some of the many areas you could look to for a capable team of board members. Pay them fairly for their work, and come to the board meetings with one or two questions or strategies they can help with. Get people who have been successful with whatever you are heading toward, and take their advice seriously. Let your leadership team learn from them and lean on them for help. But most importantly, invite them to critique your leadership, your strategy, and your vision and take action on their feedback.

CHAPTER 2

BUSINESS BOOKS—READ 'EM ALL

Sent: July 4, 12:30 p.m.
From: CEO
To: Executive Team
Subject: New Book - How to Be Great Again

Everyone,

Just finished this great new book about how to be great again, and we should use it as our new mantra. It beats Good to Great hands down. Set up a mandatory company meeting for tomorrow so I can share my insights with everyone.

So that we're all on the same page, please read the book before the meeting.

This will be great!

Your CEO

The key to great leadership is to make sure you are up on all the latest literature. You don't actually need to read the books, but you have to act like you did. You want to have your desk full of unread books, and if anyone asks, you loved this one or that one, but say things like "It was insightful," "It changed my world view," or some other mindless statement that will convey your brilliance. Remember, you can bluff your way to greatness—just look at all the leaders before you!

Then the key is to shame your direct reports into reading books and then take whatever ideas they come up with and pretend they were yours. Say things like "Why don't you give it a read and tell me what you think; then we'll see if we agree." Then, no matter what they say, always disagree with something because you need to be right. Remember, that's key to great leadership.

Of course you'll have to agree with something, so let them sweat it out for a while and when something strikes your fancy, pounce! Say, "That's exactly what I thought! How do you think we should best implement that?" And no matter what they say, respond with "Just what I was thinking. Let me give it some more thought and get back to you."

Then—here comes the really brilliant part—wait a day or two and then send out a note to the team, taking that idea. Now you own it and can assign the hapless manager to implement *your* plan. Brilliant! No one will be the wiser.

Remember not to use the same person twice because there is a slim possibility that someone may catch on, so spread it around a little.

Another great way to never have to read an actual book is to have your executive team read them first, write CliffsNotes versions of the books, and then collectively decide the best way forward. This will create a feeding frenzy for your attention, so, again, you get to be brilliant and never have to crack a book!

If the idea bombs, you now have a scapegoat to blame, keeping your hands clean of all culpability for a bad idea. And if it's a good one and your team actually makes something work, you swoop into the meeting and praise everyone for implementing your idea so well and to your specifications. It's a win-win for you!

If you don't have a big team of minions to assign the actual reading to, just go on Amazon and read a review or two, then copy and paste them together as your idea and assign it to one of your people. Again, no one will ever check to see if you plagiarized anything from Amazon, I mean really, who reads those?! Always go for the books that have lots of reviews so you can go with the crowd.

LET'S GET REAL

Not every business book is worth reading, and just because you read it doesn't mean it's a great one. What are the problems your organization is facing? Find relevant books so you can connect the dots for your people. Books are one way to teach and train your teams, but today there are so many other ways you can utilize as well. TED Talks, podcasts, blogs, speakers, and generally anything that addresses the challenges or opportunities you are facing in the organization—these can bring the conversation to life and make it feel more real for your team.

Find the useful nuggets in each book and paraphrase. Let those who want to read the whole book read it if, and only if, there is value for the entire team and the company.

CHAPTER 3

THE BEAUTY IN THE REARVIEW MIRROR

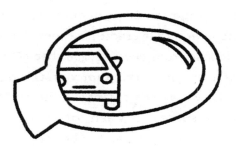

(NOTE TO SELF: ARRIVE LATE TO MEETINGS AND MAKE AN ENTRANCE—IT'S YOUR SHOW!)

Sent: July 5, 10:30 p.m.
From: CEO
To: Executive Team
Subject: Unacceptable Results

I want to express my disgust at the results we've been having lately. I'm shocked that you have gone so far down from last quarter. We need some new plans, and I want to go back to what was working last quarter and last year. Enough of this new innovative stuff.

We'll meet first thing (9:00) tomorrow morning, and each of you should have a plan that will work.

Your CEO

Remember, you are in charge and what you say goes. If some-one wants to take off in a new, untested direction, why the hell should you go with them? It's not their nuts on the table. Well, technically it's not your nuts either, because it's all from your trust fund, and there's more where that came from...

But back to the point. The best ideas are always those that have worked in the past—there is nothing new to be learned from trying something new. So drag out those old plans, put a new shine on them, and take credit for them all over again! You have plenty to choose from because, just between us, you have some pretty smart people working for you. Of course, all credit goes to you because we wouldn't want anyone getting too uppity!

The real key to success is wash, rinse, and repeat. And if you get stuck in the spin cycle, all the better!

Take a look at a good quarter or year and see what it was you did that worked. Then drag that strategy out of the closet and run it again. If it was a promotion that went well, do it again! It won't matter that you just did it and made it special so that customers who purchased will feel a little jilted now that you are running it again—you want all those who didn't purchase it before! Remember, you can make anything look new again. Just look in the mirror and see how good you look now compared to last year!

Once you've gathered the team together and shamed them for their poor performance, listen to their ideas. Make sure you've already thought of a surefire winner from past success-es, and summarily dismiss all their ideas and share yours as the one you've decided on. Even if it's eerily similar to someone else's on the team, be sure to note one key difference—even if you make it up—that makes yours superior. Keep in mind that leadership is all about you leading, so it needs to be your idea, your strategy, and your say-so. The team is just there to execute.

The beauty of this plan is that you have a high likelihood

of success and if you fail, it's the team's fault, based on their execution; therefore, once again, you are golden! One key element is that you tolerate no dissent whatsoever. If someone questions you, take them out immediately with a put-down so fierce that no one else will have the balls to question you. You'll feel great about yourself, and the rest of the team will be awed by your strong leadership.

Remember, looking backward is really looking forward, again! (Note to self: Put that in my book as a brilliant quote.)

LET'S GET REAL

Looking in the rearview mirror for insights is a good thing. *Only* looking in the rearview mirror will cause a serious accident. Take the insights and build a better plan forward; don't be afraid to innovate; and for God's sake, listen to your people. They often do have the best ideas. The best approach to gaining insight from the past is to talk about what went well, what did not go well, and what you will do next time. If you don't learn from past mistakes, you will be doomed to repeat them. Get in the habit of doing a mini debrief after every plan, implementation, project, initiative, or action. Not only will you get better each time, but you'll also be teaching your team a great strategy for speed and learning.

CHAPTER 4

SOLO STRATEGY: ALWAYS BE THE SAGE ON THE STAGE

CEO'S KEYNOTE SPEECH ANNUAL COMPANY MEETING

"Good morning, everyone! Welcome to this year's all-company meeting! What a great way to start the year, by bringing everyone together and charting our course for a successful year. We are going to meet our goals this year—and in the next couple of hours, I'll be telling you what those goals are and what I expect you to do to achieve them.

"As you all know, I have always had an amazing vision for this company, a vision that only I could have since it's the vision that I first had as a young boy, and it's that vision that's fueled my passion for achieving the success that you are all challenged to create for me now.

"My vision is going to change the world. My vision is going to change the way every single person on the planet does business. My vision will attract world-class talent, catapult our industry into the future, and shatter our competition, leaving us so far ahead of the pack it will take decades for other industry sectors to catch up. Who's with me?

"I want you to know that I have been working tirelessly over the last two weeks to dot every *i* and cross every *t* to make sure my strategic plan is bulletproof. I have developed innovations in product development, a roadmap for total digital transformation, and a workforce enablement plan that is truly groundbreaking. And I can tell that you all are as excited as I am!

"But there's no time to lose. We've got to get started right away on executing my plan. You each have an extremely important role in my plan's success. On your chairs today, you'll find a very good business book called "Cog in the Machine." It's about how important each individual job is and how the goals of that job contribute to the larger strategy of the founder—me. I want you to read it this weekend, and on Monday be ready to get your assignment from your managers about the goals I've created for you.

"Next year at this time, I will be revealing my vision, and we will unveil all you've done to make it a reality. Onward and upward! Go, team, go!"

Now here's a great example of a visionary leader! He knows where he's going, why he's going there, and how he's going to get there, which is what strategic leadership is all about. Keeping the staff in the dark on those three things will make it happen even faster—fewer questions, fewer detractors, and certainly no one thinking that they have a better idea that yours.

Remember, it was your idea in the first place and without you, there would be no them. Employees come and go and will never be as invested in your business as you are, and they certainly will never have the kind of groundbreaking strategic innovations that you do. No one else is as qualified and experienced to set strategic direction for your company for one simple reason: it's your company—you thought of it first!

The other reason to keep your strategic thoughts to yourself is that there's little chance that most employees are even smart enough to know what you are talking about. This is why good leaders keep their P&Ls secret. Most people are too dumb to understand them, and nobody really needs to know how the business makes money anyway. The same holds true for strategic plans. Developing them on your own and keeping them a secret spares your employees the embarrassment of being incapable of contributing to them.

Solo strategizing is also important for remaining competitive. You certainly wouldn't want one of your star managers to know where you envision the company being in five years, and then to share that information with your biggest competitor! So remember, keep them guessing, tell them the minimum they need to know to get the job done, and you'll be well on your way to success.

LET'S GET REAL

Strategy is not a solo sport. Period.

Sadly, the example above is far too common, with entrepreneurs and leaders who believe that they, and they alone, are the innovative brain and strategic brawn behind the business and that no other person is as qualified or capable of developing or contributing to a strategic plan. More often than not, they also believe that it was their genius that led the business to success or growth, when the reality is that luck and timing probably played a much bigger part than one individual's intellect or creativity.

This is not to say that entrepreneurs and leaders don't have great ideas; they do, and they are also often more risk tolerant than others. But good, solid strategic plans that can be put into action and lead to specific results take teamwork, collaboration, shared vision, and contribution from the best and brightest. An idea may germinate with you, but unless you allow for further development or evolution of that idea through inclusion and motivation of your management team and staff, you are setting a course for strategic disaster.

Many entrepreneurs and leaders fall into this trap not out of arrogance but out of fear and insecurity. Just because you are the founder, the CEO, or the leader doesn't mean you have to have the big idea. It means you have to empower others to bring their ideas forward or to evolve ideas into better ones.

CHAPTER 5

PUNCHED IN THE GUT

CEO NOTES
Journal Entry
July 1

Today I was pretty pleased with myself. I just had this feeling that if I stuck to my guns, I would be right, and of course I was. It's really hard to teach gut instinct to all these wannabes coming up behind me—either you have it or you don't. And I've got it in spades.

As per our corporate overlord's decree, we embarked on our annual strategic planning exercise—really more of a check-in on what did or didn't happen the previous year—but for the sake of our underlings, we call it strategic planning. As always, we're on track for big bonuses as a result of my leadership—I have this thing nailed. We went through the list of all of last year's projects, and not only are they on track but they are also set to net bigger profits than anticipated and likely to be done early. I was quick to point out that without my intervention last year, we may not have gone down this road; so thanks to my 100 percent right track record of "gut," we nailed it. They gave me a round of applause that was a little weaker than I would have expected due to my leadership and the results, but no matter, at least they are recognizing it.

Then we started talking about the product strategy for the coming year and the need to refresh some of the older products, which, ironically, were selling like crazy. My gut was telling me that this retro trend was responsible for the increase in sales of these dinosaurs, so why mess with a good thing? The product manager started blathering on about compatibility to the latest technology, et cetera, and I just held up a hand and cut him off. He had all sorts of charts and data to back up his ideas, but let's be clear: my gut trumps that crap all day long. Were we not just looking at the unchallenged success of my gut instincts from last year? Sometimes I really wonder how dumb these guys are. Oh well, that's good for me because I'll never have to worry about any of these signposts challenging me for my job.

The conversation got pretty quiet when I said we'd be continuing to take advantage of the retro trend, so no need for any product updates in the line in question. Of course, I did the CEO thing and pretended to care, so I asked for any differing opinions. To my surprise, the numb-nuts who had all that data raised his hand and started to object. Jesus, I guess he thought I really meant it when I asked for differing opinions; not my fault the idiot wants to commit career suicide. I shut him down by telling him that my gut has gotten me this far in life and it was going to get me a lot farther than his stupid data. Well, that shut him down.

So once again, I was able to use my trusty gut to guide our "strategy" to success and the team was impressed with my acumen and smarts. Let the bonuses roll in!

CEO NOTES
Journal Entry
September 26

OK, so I really hate to admit this, but that dumbass product manager might have been correct with his stupid data. The product line is sinking like the Titanic, threatening to put our entire budget in the red for the year and possibly even next year. This means my bonus will be cut in half and the rest of the team will get nothing—but it's kind of their fault for not seeing this. My gut has never failed me before, so I'm really not sure what happened here. There must have been some market condition that changed or was out of our control, or possibly the knowledge was unavailable, causing this to go south.

Now I need to figure out how to blame it on something or someone else because I'm not giving up that my gut is always right. And I want that bonus. Competitors? New technology? Market saturation? Coolness of retro cooled off faster than I thought—make that faster than anyone could possibly have predicted? Yep, that's the ticket because the first three were what that doofus product manager with the data told me, so I'll go with the last one and point to some others who were caught in the same spot. I can spin this because it's actually true—it's not my fault, my gut is still the ticket to success, and it was completely out of my control! Gut instinct is a leader's best friend—at least it's mine.

LET'S GET REAL

While there is a lot of research to suggest that "gut instinct" can be a good guidance system to follow, it doesn't mean you should do so without any research or facts to back you up when it comes to strategy. That's just reckless and likely to result in failure. Or, like our hapless CEO, it's vanity. Good leaders who listen to their gut use a "trust but verify" method, not the "my way or the highway" method. Ignoring all evidence to the contrary will punch you in the gut every time.

The other thing that got our CEO into trouble was his big ego. One or two correct guesses or gut instincts that turn out well do not make a faultless gut. It means your gut may have had some good feelings and you probably got lucky. Humility is a good thing when it comes to getting things right. Experience, gut, luck, and DATA will keep you on the straight and narrow every time—and you won't need to go in for a "gut check" when you fail.

CHAPTER 6

WAGGING THE DOG

Sent: July 5, 8:35 a.m.
From: CEO
To: All Staff
Subject: NEW! Collaboration Tools

Good morning, everyone!

I hope everyone had a fun and festive holiday weekend. Welcome back!

As we are now moving into the second quarter of the year, I wanted to touch base on a couple of important things.

First, we made great progress on our annual strategic goals! We are just a couple of months behind on the product development work stream, but I think if we really put our noses to the grindstone here in the second quarter, together we can make it happen. As you all know, product development is absolutely our most important goal this year, as we're sure to get dusted by the competition if we don't start next year with at least four new products on the shelf! So it's crunch time for sure.

Second, I want to announce that we've made an exciting new investment in technology and are going to be introducing an entirely new platform of collaboration tools. I know we have a lot going on in the second half, but it's super exciting and we spent a ton of money on them, so we're going to need to put our strategic plans on hold for about six to nine weeks while we get the new platform integrated. We'll lose some time, but we can make it up in the fall, right? Go, team!

I know I told you all that product development takes precedence over everything else we tackle this year, but our biggest competitor is using this new collaboration tool; and if they can make time to get it installed, train everyone, and be fully operational in a year, so can we! And we have already paid the vendor and the license fees, so it's happening—starting on Monday!

Your CEO

Annual strategic plan not going quite as well as you thought it would? Feeling behind or being eclipsed by the competition? Don't get mad, get distracted! One of the best ways to take attention off of the fact that you have failed to lead your organization to strategic success is to throw something super tactical and strategically useless into the mix! Trendy technology is the absolute poster child for big distractions and can be used by the staff as a perfect excuse for why they didn't meet their personal business objectives.

You can create mountains of distractions simply by introducing a big, new technology solution. You'll have to create teams for developing requirements; bring in a super-distracting vendor team to interrupt everyone's workday for a couple of months; create teams for focus groups; and shut down your current servers, website, email, etc. And if all goes according to your plan, it will take twice as long and cost twice as much as you'd hoped. Now you have a full-blown four-alarm fire to deal with, and your strategic plan will be forever lost and forgotten. This won't be remembered as the year you blew your strategic goals; it will be remembered as the year you got saddled with that awful vendor! *Whew! Winning!*

Another method for taking attention away from a failing strategic initiative is to shine a big, bright light on your poorest-performing employee. You can saddle them with so much responsibility for executing said strategic plan that they become an incredibly valuable scapegoat when things don't go according to plan. And in this case, this won't be remembered as the year you blew your strategic goals; it will be remembered as the year you should have fired that train-wreck employee much sooner than you did. You just couldn't because of your huge heart. *Whew! Winning!* Plus the martyr card gets played!

LET'S GET REAL

Strategies aren't projects, and they don't get put on hold.

Strategy and strategic direction are long-term commitments about the direction a company is headed, and your job is to keep it headed in that (general) direction and not let it get interrupted, blown off course, or, worst of all, forgotten about entirely. Leaders will often knowingly or unknowingly allow or create other activities within the organization that quickly eclipse any attention or discussion of the grander plan.

When this happens, perhaps you should ask yourself if you created this distraction because it's easier or has a clearer outcome, or to blame the strategy's failure on someone other than yourself. Perhaps you created or allowed it because your strategic initiatives aren't going to plan and you can't see a way to get them back on track.

Or...perhaps you just can't walk and chew gum at the same time.

Any way you slice it, the lesson here is that all businesses need a strategic plan, and all leaders need to first focus themselves on that plan, then ensure that everyone in the organization is focused on the same plan. Aligning the people, processes, and, yes, even the platforms to that plan is what drives the business forward. It is not something that you put on hold, and it's certainly not something that you trade for some other tactical initiative. Strategic direction is what you focus on and what gives you purpose.

CHAPTER 7

MAGIC 8 BALL

"IDEAS CAN COME FROM ANYWHERE," SPEECH FROM THIS YEAR'S CEO ROUNDTABLE:

"I've always found that I like to get ideas from everywhere— even random people can often give me a perspective that helps me clarify the situation, and therefore the answer. My leadership philosophy is that I gather the best ideas, pick one, and then execute—as all the best leadership books will tell you. Let's take a recent example.

"I knew we needed to reinvent or at the very least shake up our HR department. It was a complete and total mess. So I gathered all the executives into a meeting and asked for ideas about what a structure that would work better for the firm might look like. Of course, they wanted to go into elaborate detail about what wasn't working before we decided on a strategy, but I wanted to be decisive and just get the mess cleaned up before it started sticking to me like glue. So I shut that conversation down and asked for ideas to fix it.

"Reluctantly, they all gave some ideas; some were terrible, but a couple in there were worth consideration. After eliminating the really stupid or costly ideas, we decided to rework the department, hire a more senior VP to run the division, and create some clear-cut objectives that the department needs to achieve over the next year. Everyone left the room feeling pretty good about it, and I must say I felt pretty good about my leadership through a potential crisis.

"The following day I had a lunch with some fellow CEOs—we meet up at least once a month to catch up and share ideas—and I shared my HR story. We had a few great laughs about the HR leader who left and also my shutting down the discussion about what went wrong—who needs to listen to all that whining! One of the guys had a great idea to just outsource the whole damn thing. He said that HR is so transferable these days that outsourcing it is a great way to save money and get rid of the "people" headache that it creates.

"I was a little skeptical about how that might work with over five hundred people in the company, but he assured me it was the only way to go. His fifty-person company was running better than ever with an outsourced model. He called it outsourcing the whining! I liked the sound of that!

"Later that day I was getting a haircut, and I really enjoy getting perspective from my stylist; he's a great guy and hears so much that I always get a piece of wisdom from him. He thought it was a great idea and even had a suggestion for the firm: one of his clients! This idea was really coming together, so when he offered to make the introduction, I was all over it. I followed up with a call to the CEO, and we had a great talk. She had never worked with a firm as large as ours before, but was confident it would be no problem, and she was completely staffed up to do so!

"The next morning, I sent out the following email to the Senior Executive Team:

Team:

Although we had a great meeting yesterday and came up with some good solutions, I've been talking to a few people and come up with a better strategy. Let's outsource the entire department. No need to have this expensive department in-house; it's just a headache and a burden. I've asked HR Outfitters to give us a quote, and I'm convinced it's the way to go.

Rod, I've CC'd you on the email to HR Outfitters, so go ahead and get that contract executed ASAP.

Susan, can you work up the list of people in the department we'll need to let go and get that over to HR Outfitters so they can do the layoffs? No point in us doing it.

"Of course, there was some grumbling about the new strategy, but as a leader it's your job to be open to new ideas, wherever they might come from. I feel confident that by going to seemingly random sources, the solutions can be better than what the team came up with in the first place!

"Questions?"

LET'S GET REAL

Getting outside perspectives is always a good idea. Using that information to override your team without their input is usually a recipe for a giant face-plant. Unfortunately, leaders do this on a regular basis. Ever heard of the leader who only listens to the last person he spoke with, so the team always tries to be the last one in line so their idea is the winner?

Sometimes a problem cannot be solved with the same level of thinking that created it in the first place. In that instance, it's the leader's job to encourage the team—not the leader—to think out of the box. The team always needs to be involved in the solution, or it will be dead on arrival. How invested in the new HR outsource strategy do you think the team of our blockheaded CEO's company is? Not only will they not be invested in making it a success, they will likely do all they can to sabotage it.

Great leaders encourage the team to look at outside contributors for ideas, not just the leader. Then everyone can get back together to decide on the right strategy. Those leaders who are always looking outside of the team and change direction more often than a feather in the wind end up with mediocre solutions and disengaged teams. Leaders who encourage the team to think out of the box and to own and implement their own solutions will have much better outcomes than our fickle leader who puts as much stock in his Magic 8 Ball as he does his own leadership team.

CHAPTER 8

SNAKE OIL STRATEGY

GOOOOOOOOOOOOOD **MORNING!** WELCOME TO THIS YEAR'S ANNUAL STRATEGIC PLANNING SESSION! GRAB SOME COFFEE—HURRY UP, WAKE UP, RISE AND SHINE, PEOPLE! GRAB A SEAT, NOTEBOOKS OUT, THINKING CAPS ON—WE ARE GOING TO GET STRATEGIC! MY NAME IS BOB, I AM WITH BOB CAMPBELL CONSULTING INCORPORATED, I AM YOUR LEAD STRATEGIC CONSULTANT, AND IT'S DAMN NICE TO MEET YOU! I AM AN ACCOMPLISHED STRATEGIC CONSULTANT! I AM ALSO A MOTIVATIONAL SPEAKER! I HAVE WRITTEN TWO BOOKS, WHICH WILL BE AVAILABLE FOR YOU TO PURCHASE AFTER TODAY'S SESSION!

I want to extend a BIG HUG OF THANKS to your BRILLIANT founder and CEO for hiring ME, BOB, THE STRATEGIC CONSULTANT, to take you on this EXCITING JOURNEY today!

Now SIT DOWN! You'll find in front of you, on this table, TOYS! So grab a toy and start PLAYING WITH IT! We are going to have twenty minutes of PLAYTIME to get your creative juices flowing. Get those big ideas rolling through the cobwebs of your busy brains, and by the end of the day, we are going to have the MOST BRILLIANT STRATEGY YOU'VE EVER SEEN! Am I excited? HELL YES I'm excited!

...

PLAYTIME IS OVER! Now we are going to BONDING TIME! I want you to look to your left, and now to your right. Give one of the two people sitting next to you a HUGE HUG! Come on now—WITH FEELING! Now doesn't that feel better? We are going to be honest, vulnerable, real, and, dammit, you people are going to shine today! I can already spot the rock stars in the room. I have a sixth sense for strategy, I tell you—I know exactly who the real contributors are in this company. I can tell just by LOOKING AT YOU!

Now SIT DOWN and open your BOB CAMPBELL CONSULT-ING INCORPORATED notebooks, provided by ME, BOB CAMP-BELL. Pens ready! OK! For the next thirty minutes we are going to have THINKING TIME! I want each and every one of you to write down your TOP FIFTY GOALS for the year. You have thirty minutes, people. HOP TO IT! I am going to step out of the room, grab some coffee at the Starbucks in the lobby, and will be back in exactly twenty-eight minutes. EYES DOWN!

...

CONGRATULATIONS, team! You've accomplished step one of MY proprietary strategic consulting M-E-T-H-O-D-O-L-O-G-Y. That's what I do—I have a method, and I'm practically a doctor in methodology! And I'm pretty funny too, if I do say so my-self. Now I want you to circle your three favorite goals, your top three, not the most important, but your favorite. One, two, three, GO! When you're done, put the paper in the basket. PUT

THE PAPER IN THE BASKET! And because I've been doing this for forty years, and because of my sixth strategic sense, I am going to draw five of your goals lists out of this basket. One, two, three, four, five. YOU! What's your name? Get up here; let's see what you've got when you're in the hot seat, pal. Here, take these five pages, and I want you to choose ONE GOAL from each of these pages and write them on the whiteboard. One from each—that's five total, sport.

And there you go! THERE THEY ARE! Your top five goals for the year. THE BOB CAMPBELL WAY! This is a democracy, people! And LOOK AT YOU! You did it! You've identified the top five things that your company is going to focus on this year whether you want to or not. I knew you had it in you! NOW LET'S HAVE LUNCH!

LET'S GET REAL

We have all suffered through at least one planning session facilitated by a "professional facilitator" that had some aspect of this nightmare scenario to it, whether it's the overly enthusiastic stranger who claims to be "as passionate about your brand as you are" or the pile of sticky and well-used fidget toys to play with. We've all seen part of Bob's big strategy charade. The "methodology" that they pitch as their own proprietary genius varies little from consultant to consultant, and the results are seldom better than what you might get out of a five-minute multiple-choice survey.

Many leaders dread the obligatory annual strategic-planning session because (a) it brings the otherwise productive management team to a screeching halt for an entire day; (b) they themselves have no idea how to facilitate a session to yield actionable results; or (c) by the end of the first quarter—as is with many businesses—everything has changed and the planning you did during that wasted day-long session goes right out the window. And the crumpled sheets of paper from the big notepad easel generated on that dreary January day of being locked in a room—with a two-week holiday hangover—sit until about July; then you finally decide to toss them in the recycle bin along with the rest of your best-laid plans.

Strategic planning is not an exercise or a box to check every year. Real strategic planning is also not for the unengaged or faint of heart. It's for the real contributors in your business, and it's up to you to make sure it's eye-opening, useful, and has real material impact on how you operate the business in the coming year. Great leaders know that planning for the planning session is as important as the planning session itself, and if done correctly—with or without a qualified and well-vetted consultant—a good planning session is not an event, it's a progressive mind-shift that will be felt throughout the organization.

A few tips to get it right:

- Consider having at least four planning sessions throughout the year. Things change. You're moving at the speed of business.

- Gather feedback and ideas from your participants *before* a planning meeting, not after.

- Spend as much time talking about what you are going to *stop* doing and what went wrong as you do about what you are going to *start* doing. Good on top of bad is still bad.

- Operationalize your goals and strategies throughout the business, to every employee, every day. Make it matter.

- And most importantly: LISTEN. Let conversations evolve.

If you're doing it right, you should hear some things that you haven't or didn't want to hear before.

SECTION 2

IT'S ALL IN THE EXECUTION(ER?)

Now it's getting fun. You've spent a ton of time and money planning, and now you actually get to do something other than sit around and hope something will happen—you get to make it happen. Feel those butterflies? Or is it just the sinking feeling that maybe the plan you created might go the way of the Titanic because you forgot to plan for the inevitable iceberg that has your name on it? What? You didn't do a SWOT (strengths, weaknesses, opportunities, threats)? No worries, it's very unlikely that scenario would ever play out...or would it?

The execution of a bad plan leads to a poetically tragic strategy—like having your wife and girlfriend leave you at the same time and then finding out they are lovers. As a leader, it was your job to launch this strategy rocket with a well-prepared team. It was your job to let them know exactly what, where, and when they were supposed to act. Did you make it clear who was on first? Leaders fail all the time at execution—and it's usually because they are the chief executioner.

Plans fail in the execution stage because they are a wash, rinse, and repeat of the previous year's plan—not some big innovation—drawing a big yawn and a "who cares" from the team who has to do the work. Copying another company's execution strategy will not make a bad plan work well; it will only create more confusion and chaos. The leader who refuses to switch tracks despite the oncoming train will likely be flattened.

Then there are those leaders who read the latest business books and adopt the made-up words to describe what everyone already knows, and thinks they are the reincarnation of Steve Jobs. Or the leader who takes SMART goals to such an extreme that the changing of the bathroom tissue is charted daily so that even the janitor gets to participate in the execution of the planning process. As those involved in dangerous sports often find out, taking things to extremes has a nasty habit of resulting in death. That's when the leader of execution becomes the executioner.

These are just some of the many ways that the execution of a plan makes for great how-not-to stories. If you want to avoid some of the most obvious pratfalls when it comes to executing the most beautifully crafted strategy, keep reading. You'll likely see some of your "friends" in these stories.

CHAPTER 9

INNOVATION IS FOR LOSERS

Sent: Sunday, March 3, 7:42 p.m.
From: David, Founder & CEO
To: Chris, Director of IT
Subject: Web Sight Budget

Chris,

I've been putting a lot of thought into our technology budget for this year, and I'm having second thoughts about your request to redo our web sight.

When we started the company in 2002, we paid a lot of money to an Internet developer to build our web sight. He made sure it was compatible with browsers like Netscape and Internet Explorer and also made sure it looked good on all different sizes of computers. He did a great job. In fact, even when I look at it today on my iPad it looks pretty good.

I also think the designer template he used still looks good. Maybe we could make the logo a little bigger and use up some of the white space with more copy, but, all in all, it works and looks good on my computer.

I don't really understand why you think it needs to be updated. It seems to be taking payments OK through PayPal, and when I type in our company name in the Google it comes right up. I also don't understand why you think it's crucial that people be able to look at our web sight on their telephones. Everything would be so small. Why would someone want to do that?

I know you are going to say that 18 years is too long to go without a refresh, especially now that we only sell our products on the Internet, but you know me, Chris. I'm an "if it ain't broke don't fix it" kind of guy.

Dave

Sent: Monday, March 4, 7:00 a.m.
From: Chris, Director of IT
To: David, Founder & CEO
Subject: RE: Web Sight Budget

Good morning, Dave.

Sorry for the short notice, but I wanted to let you know that Friday was my last day and I won't be coming in today, or any other day. Good luck.

Chris

LET'S GET REAL

First of all, if you have a founder or CEO who uses terms like "web sight," that should be the first clue that you're dealing with someone who is grossly incompetent and should have retired a decade or three ago.

But all kidding aside, if you are a leader or business owner who doesn't understand the importance of technology in every single aspect of your business, then you need to hire someone who does—immediately. Give them the biggest budget you can afford and let them do their job. Technology is here to stay; it should be embraced, not feared. It can be the single most powerful thing that can propel your business into the future.

Many leaders are casual users or late adopters of technology, or their foray into technology was at a time when many of the tools, platforms, and apps available online felt "free." There was a time when the do-it-yourself attitude prevailed, and they don't understand that now, more than ever, the you-get-what-you-pay-for theory rings true.

Embracing technology is just one part of having an innovative mind-set, however. Being innovative means you are willing to evolve, to change, to rethink the methods of the past and seek out new ideas that are more relevant to today. Innovation isn't an initiative; it's a way of thinking and a mode of operating that is always on and ever present.

Today, "moving at the speed of business" means embracing innovation in everything we do and being open to the fluid business environment that it creates. Great leaders are avid readers, continuously learning how they can take what is happening in the world and in our culture and use this as a platform of ideas for how to evolve their businesses.

The best-laid plans need to have innovation at their core and a "take a step and repeat" approach for long-term planning by continually innovating. "Next year we are going to do something we've never done before" is a perfectly reasonable goal when it means we are going to innovate and push ourselves to think outside of our comfort zone.

Leaders who stay comfortable—who hold on to what they know best—or who refuse to invest in innovation, even at the most basic level, will inevitably get left behind in a small, irrelevant cloud of dust.

CHAPTER 10

BY IMITATION ONLY

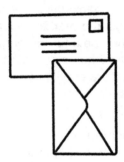

Sent: August 18, 11:00 a.m.
From: Ann, CEO
To: Dan, Director of Marketing
Subject: NWFFPSC Booth

Dan,

Last year at the National Worldwide Forum for the Future of Professional Services & Consulting, I saw at least twenty of our direct competitors with booths that were far superior to ours. It made us look like some podunk, rinky-dink small business staffed by a bunch of hacks with AAs from the local community college, trying to compete with the Zeuses and Adonises of Big Consulting. I mean, honestly, are you going to try to tell me that we are going to steal market share when we show up to our biggest industry trade show looking like we did?

Bonafide Consulting had a 50' x 50' booth with a coffee bar, a barista, finger sandwiches, and four parchment-leather sofas to schmooze their potential clients. Hat Trick Services had a full-blown movie theater showing their commercials on a nonstop loop, with a popcorn vendor and an endless supply of KitKats—I mean come on, we didn't even have a water cooler in our booth! And if that wasn't embarrassing enough, Premier One Fair Equity was prancing around touting free martinis at their open-invitation happy hour, and they hired Toto—yes, the band, not the dog. Argh!

Dan, this year I want you to kill it at NWFFPSC! I want to bury the competition with our booth presence. Last year we spent $25,000 on our booth for a three-day show. This year, I'm throwing in an additional $10,000 because I want you to blow them out of the water. I want a booth that is on a corner or smack dab in the middle of the trade-show floor. I want our entire sales-and-marketing staff to be there, and they are not allowed to leave the booth for more than one bathroom break. That means they stay put for 7 hours and 55 minutes—the more people we have at our booth, the more popular we'll look. No uniforms, shirts, or name tags because we want them to look like potential customers. Just pack 'em in there.

I would also like to see some sort of very loud and showy entertainment. Last year, Bonanza Consulting had four beautiful "booth babes" in short skirts and four-inch heels demonstrating the latest in artificial intelligence for cloud computing. We don't do AI, but it's the hot new thing, and I want us to look like we are on the absolute bleeding edge of technology. So figure out what AI is and make it happen, Dan. Make. It. Happen.

I'm not going to take another gloating call from that crusty old Harold Sherman at Bonanza asking me if we've had budget cuts for NWFF-PSC. Total humiliation from one of our biggest competitors. No way is that happening to ME again, and it's YOUR job to make sure of it. So get to work. I expect a plan and booth layout on my desk by next week.

Urgently,

Ann, CEO

Now here's someone who really knows how to stick it to the competition! Paralyzed by fear of not keeping up, she's got her right-hand man Dan on a mission to out-do every one of her overspending, overindulging, glitzy competitors at the next big event so she'll look brighter, bigger, better, and—well, let's face it—smarter!

Ann knows that it's all about keeping up with the competition, and her strategy is spot-on. She keeps copious notes on their advertising and marketing, she peppers her customers with questions about her competitors, and she's even been known to poke around for confidential documents and proposals to see if she can get "competitive intelligence." Her marketing team spends hours and hours doing competitive analysis reports for her, and her recruiting team stalks every one of her top competitors' senior employees on LinkedIn, so she knows exactly who they are and what they are doing.

Nothing is going to get by Ann. She proudly refers to herself as ruthlessly competitive, and she'll go to the ends of the earth to make sure her competitors know it.

LET'S GET REAL

Our CEO Ann is not ruthlessly competitive; she's scared to death to face the fact that her business's strategy, core offerings, and customer testimonials simply aren't good enough to compete. Her insecurity about where her business falls in line next to her competitors causes her to spend more energy chasing the competition than she does creating her own compelling strategy.

We see this every day in copycat marketing, and if you look closely, you'll see it right down to copycat headlines. Social strategies have compounded the problem with increased messages to market and trends that change so fast that businesses are executing social marketing without even knowing if it works. Panic sets in when Ann sees her competitors tweeting twenty times a day, so she runs like her hair is on fire through the marketing department demanding a Twitter strategy without knowing or even thinking about results.

We see this in product strategy as well. Beware the leader who sees a competitor launch a new product strategy one day and demands a company-wide rebrand the next day. It's not to say that being competitive isn't important or that keeping an eye on your competitors isn't time well spent—it is. But great businesses are built by leaders who have confidence in their vision and spend more time executing that vision than they do chasing the competition. Customers buy confidence, investors invest in businesses that are sure of themselves, and great talent is attracted to differentiated workplaces.

Rest assured that Ann may be pleased with her glitzy booth next year, but it won't bear fruit for the business. It will just be a doom loop of one-upmanship year after year. And meanwhile, a smart, stealthy competitor with a confident, sharp strategy will come from behind and blow them all out of the water without spending one dime on a trade-show booth.

CHAPTER 11

THE SABOTEUR

Sent: April 14, 2:00 p.m.
From: Gayle, CEO
To: Robert, Director of Product Strategy
Subject: Rethinking Annual Plan

Robert,

As we turn the corner on the third quarter here, I wanted to touch base on our annual product-rollout plan. I know the big launch is already planned for the fourth quarter, and we're depending on holiday sales to help push us over our sales goal, but I'm having some second thoughts.

I know you spent the better part of last year with the research firm. We did spend a fair amount of money on market research, and there was consensus in the focus groups, but I'm just not sure it's the direction we should be heading.

I had dinner with one of the principals at the private-equity firm where my boyfriend works (it's his boss, actually), and I explained our annual strategy and product-rollout plan, and he thinks we are on the wrong track.

I didn't have a lot of time to go over the research findings, but I explained it in summary. He thinks that our competitors are just doing a better job of pushing new product into the market and maybe we should consider putting more energy into the products we have.

He's not in our target market and doesn't use our products or our competitors' products, but he is a private-equity guy and really smart. He's in their professional services division, so he doesn't really have any expertise in CPG. But again, he's a private-equity guy and is all about the money, and he thinks we are spending too much money on market research and I should just trust my gut.

My gut says that we've come this far with the products we have, so why not do more of what we know how to do and what we know will be successful? I mean, it got us this far, right?

Gayle

Excellent plan, Gayle. This has to be super demoralizing for Robert, having spent an entire year doing market research; then presenting a thoughtful, fiscally sound, and strategic plan for success; and marching toward the incentive package you put together for him at the beginning of the year.

There's no better way to keep your team on their toes than by changing horses midstream as often and as disruptively as you can. After all, your business needs to be flexible, and your people need to be able to pivot at a moment's notice.

You're doing a fantastic job of getting solid advice from advisors as well. There's no better way to seek sage wisdom than to reach out to people who don't know your business at all—that way their opinions are completely objective. Now Robert will have plenty of time to look around at what your competitors are doing, and maybe next year you can just follow in their footsteps and skip all that spending on market research.

LET'S GET REAL

There are two important themes in this anecdote.

The first is the theme of the saboteur. This is the leader who, for one reason or another, can't commit to innovation or change and actively seeks out ways to sabotage a strategic plan at the most critical time. It stands to reason that many founders have a deep-seated fear of stepping outside the safety net of "doing things the way we always have" because that is what got their business to where it is. But this fear often rears its ugly head when change and progress are the most important factors for survival.

The second theme is good old-fashioned stick-to-what-we-know-and-make-it-happen-ness. Many entrepreneurs are impatient, want instant results, and aren't willing to stay the course of a strategic plan. Solid plans for business innovation and change take time and perseverance, which are often in short supply at the top.

Either way, leaders are usually the ones to sabotage the best-laid plans. Sabotage can come in the form of cutting budgets, under-resourcing, reacting to outside advice, or even just plain sticking their noses in where they don't belong (as we'll discuss in our next chapter, "The Monkey's Wrench").

When saboteurs at the top take aim at a strategic direction or plan, look first for a lack of confidence, or insecurity. Not many leaders would admit to their management team that they are fearful of taking a big step, but they all hold the power to make decisions to prevent that step from occurring. They have at their disposal a myriad of methods to sabotage a perfectly laid plan without anyone being the wiser.

If this is you, ask yourself what you're afraid of. Is the plan not well rationalized or not rationalized to your satisfaction?

Do you need to take a step back and ask for more research or evidence? Or do you need to simply come clean with your team and tell them you're having second thoughts and don't know where they are coming from? Either way, come clean before you inadvertently (or purposely) use sabotage as a cover-up for something else that's making you question where your business is headed.

If you are on the pointy end of the saboteur's stick, and your leader is actively undermining what he or she directed you to do in the first place, don't just sit by and let it happen. Even the best of leaders can find themselves in this position, and they are counting on their teams to tell them if they are being led astray. Work with your team and dig into the problem with your leader—"manage up"—and see if you can help your leader find the root cause of their fear and work through it with them.

CHAPTER 12

THE MONKEY'S WRENCH

THE INNERMOST THOUGHTS OF THE WELL-INTENTIONED CEO

It's been four months since marketing started working with that super-expensive design firm in San Francisco on that "rebranding initiative" they talked me into. I never really understood what was wrong with the logo that we have, and I certainly don't understand why we are spending 50K on a new one. My brother did the first one, and it has a special place in my heart. I'm thinking I'm going to ask them just to use a variation of the old logo and stop the bleed on the budget. I'll like it and that's what matters.

...

Sarah is the problem; I've known it all along. I seem to be the only one who thinks so, but I am looking at it from the business perspective, and I think that Doug is being too soft on her because he hired her and he likes her. She's not the right person for the job, and I think the whole lean strategy failed because of her. Everyone else thinks it's because I didn't give them enough budget, but they're wrong. If he doesn't let her go by Friday, I'm just going to do it myself and let him know on Monday.

...

I don't care what Sales says—we do not need a customer relationship management system. CRM, CRM—it's all I ever hear about from them anymore. Apparently, it's another trendy software platform they think is going to magically increase our sales tenfold. I've heard what it costs to implement one of those things, and there is no way I'm forking over that kind of cash when they can use a spreadsheet, like I always did.

...

It's our culture. We have a problem with our culture. We need to invest in some fun stuff, like ping-pong tables, and we need to hire an HR person to make sure that people are having fun here. Our culture needs to be more fun; it's the only way we are going to win the Best Places to Work award. I think I'll just go ahead and buy a couple of ping-pong tables, and we can put them in the lobby. That way our visiting clients can see how much fun we are having.

...

We need more capital. We're not growing because we don't have a treasure chest of money. I should go find some angel investors or private-equity money. Money will solve everything, and with investors on board, we'll have all of that great outside advice to help us create a winning strategy. People will love it, and we'll get so much great press.

LET'S GET REAL

Sound familiar? It's because these are some of the many random thoughts that swim aimlessly through a lot of leaders' heads during long, sleepless nights. And sometimes they act on these wayward thoughts, which more often than not then turn into giant monkey wrenches in an otherwise perfectly managed situation or a well-planned strategy.

Look, leadership can be a lonely job, and if you're a leader who believes that you, and only you, should have all the answers, or who needs to be the fixer or the solver of all the problems—it *is* lonely. But if you can look at your organization from the highest altitude possible, you'll see that there are solutions all around you. You just have to give them the space they need to come into focus.

Building a business and creating a strategy for the success of that business is a team effort that requires a wide range of talent and skills. Many entrepreneurs begin their foray into business wearing multiple hats, and they do what they need to do in order to get something off the ground. But this is not how great businesses are built, and certainly not how they thrive. Great businesses with winning strategies happen when you build a reliable team of talented people who are (a) in positions that play to their strengths, and (b) are allowed to do the jobs that you hired them to do.

Your job as a leader is not to make sure they are doing things the way you want them to; it's to make sure you've hired the right people and that they are contributing great ideas that you *hadn't* thought of, or maybe would never think of. This is a fundamental difference in an approach to management that many leaders miss entirely because they are convinced that it is indeed their job to have all the answers.

If you're a leader, ask yourself how comfortable you are answering "I don't know" to a question from one of your employees. If it makes you uncomfortable, then you have to ask yourself if you might need to work on your own skills of empowering others. The truth is, you don't have all the answers and that's why you hired them. Practice the art of empowerment by challenging those around you to bring great ideas and strategies to you, and then practice your restraint by not throwing monkey wrenches in their plans.

Great things happen when great leaders see that their job is to clear the runway for their team. You want your people to fly, not to drive planes around on the ground. And to do so, you need the view from the control tower. If you're running the airport from the tarmac, you're probably going to get hit by one of your own planes.

CHAPTER 13

SEAT ASSIGNMENTS

Sent: July 18, 10:08 a.m.
From: CEO
To: Sr. Leadership Team
Subject: Assignments for Strategic Initiatives

Team,

Great job coming up with the assignments for the six strategic initiatives from the planning session. It looks like we have all 24 mid-level managers assigned and they are split evenly—four each. Just curious if each of you is taking the lead on any of those or just letting the managers handle it?

Jon

Sent: July 18, 10:20 a.m.
From: Dana, CFO
To: CEO; Sr. Leadership Team
Subject: RE: Assignments for Strategic Initiatives

Jon,

We discussed it and decided that they really need to know how to do this, so they should learn on the job. We'll let them battle it out among themselves as to who should take the lead. We have too much on our plates as it is. They are the ones responsible for getting it done, and we'll have monthly meetings with progress updates. And the dashboard is up on the shared drive, so we'll have total visibility to check up on them.

Dana

Sent: July 18, 10:43 a.m.
From: Bob, COO
To: Dana; CEO; Sr. Leadership Team
Subject: RE: RE: Assignments for Strategic Initiatives

Concur with Dana. They've got it handled, let's move on.

Sent: July 18, 10:58 a.m.
From: CEO
To: Sr. Leadership Team
Subject: RE: RE: RE: Assignments for Strategic Initiatives

Team,

OK, if you're all on board with this, I guess it will work. I'm just a little concerned as none of them were involved last year, so not sure they'll know what we're trying to achieve. What is the plan if it goes off track?

Sent: July 18, 11:13 a.m.
From: Sarah, CMO
To: CEO; Sr. Leadership Team
Subject: RE: RE: RE: RE: Assignments for Strategic Initiatives

Jon,

Have a little faith in your senior leadership team. We know what we're doing, and this year we're just delegating a little more. The managers need to show us what they're made of—do they have the stuff or don't they? Besides, their bonuses are resting on their completion of this, so what's the problem? Good incentives, good leadership by us—it's going to work. What could possibly go wrong?

Sarah

Sent: August 18, 2:45 p.m.
From: CEO
To: Sr. Leadership Team
Subject: Update on Strat. Plan Progress

Team,

After sitting in on the monthly strat. plan meeting today, it seems pretty clear that some of these assignments were not well thought out. Who put James in charge of the marketing initiative? He just started in June, and before now his biggest marketing job was as a copywriter for a defunct newspaper.

Not to mention the person leading the HR initiative—who is she? Did I get the right idea that she's a temp and whoever you assigned in the first place opted out and a temp is now leading the selection of the new HRM software? Bob, shouldn't you be sitting in on these meetings?

I have to say, I am really getting concerned that we're not going to meet our quarterly objectives. I notice that no one has been updating the dashboard, unless it is up-to-date, and nothing has been achieved in two months?

Let me know the plan moving forward, and let's discuss in the upcoming leadership meeting on Friday.

Sent: August 18, 2:45 p.m.
From: Bob, COO
To: Sr. Leadership Team; CEO
Subject: RE: Update on Strat. Plan Progress

Jon,

We met as the Sr. leadership team and need to respectfully remind you that we are in charge of the plan. You delegated this task to us, and we have delegated it to our teams. This is an example of the type of micromanagement that you said you would not engage in anymore— we're simply trying to do what's right by the company, and you are consistently getting in the way.

We do not wish to discuss it at our meeting, and if you have any further questions, maybe we should bring the board in as we all know they signed off on the plan. Making any changes now would require them to be involved, and we all know that's not what you want, is it, Jon?

Bob

Sent: August 19, 10:12 a.m.
From: CEO
To: Sr. Leadership Team; COO
Subject: RE: RE: Update on Strat. Plan Progress

Bob,

You're right. I didn't mean to interfere, but there is a lot riding on the success of this plan. As you know, the board has said that they are looking at me as a leader and expecting better results than with our last plan. I'm just worried it's not starting off well. I'll go ahead and give it another few months to see if we have made some progress, but if you all could please put your updates on the shared drive, it would be greatly appreciated. Thank you for your help!

Jon

LET'S GET REAL

This plan is sparking into a dumpster fire. Having the right people doing the work, as well as leading the charge, has everything to do with the success of the plan itself. Execution is NOT about delegation of authority and responsibility to make the plan work; it's about giving the right initiatives, goals, and tasks to those who actually know how to do them BEST.

This leadership team is either completely derelict in their duties or trying to set the CEO up for failure. Neither is good. Good execution of the plan requires the leadership to own the strategic initiatives and to check in—not check up—to see how it's going and what is needed. Over-delegation to people who don't have a clue or are simply not skilled at the particular initiative or task will lead to chaos. Good people will leave; bad people will just quit while still on the job. Who cares anyway? The senior leadership team sure as hell didn't.

A leader who allows himself to be bullied into an execution strategy he doesn't understand or has clear doubts about is a wimp. Leadership does not need to be loud, but it does need to be strong. Allowing something you know will be a train wreck is an abdication of leadership and will doom any strategy, no matter how good.

Successful execution is about having the best people in the right roles to maximize the chances of success—not delegating it to the last man standing. Although you might be building the plane while in the air, the need for qualified mechanics is even greater than when the plane was on the ground.

CHAPTER 14

BOXERS OR BRIEFS

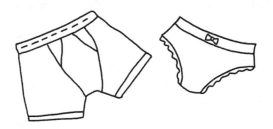

Sent: August 29, 12:44 p.m.
From: CEO
To: Companywide
Subject: Strat. Plan Decisions

Hello, everyone.

I'm very excited to announce that our leadership team has created an amazing plan for 2020! Now everyone gets to help implement it. We will be posting the plan shortly, and I hope that each and every one of you will weigh in on what you think and what role you would like to take.

Ideally, each of you will take a different section, but even if you don't, we're going to try to make sure you all get what you want. My assistant, Sarah, will be taking your preferences, and then we'll be assigning tasks based on those. With 100 of you now in the company, it will be a bit of a challenge—but not one that we haven't faced before!

And of course, I'd really like to hear what you think of the plan, because if you don't like it, that's important for us to hear. Although we went to the proverbial mountaintop to create it, we know we can't get there without you, so each and every voice is important to us. We're absolutely open to changing our course if we get enough feedback on any of the elements. Remember, every voice counts at LifeLine!

If anyone thinks of a better way to assign tasks, we are open to that too. We want to make sure everyone feels heard and that each of you is brought into the plan. Any questions are welcome; just run them through Sarah, and I'll get back to you as soon as I can.

Lastly, let me know what you think about the timing. Is it too soon? Should we stretch it out to 2021 or keep the deadline at 2020?

Thank YOU!

Steve

Sent: August 29, 2:03 p.m.
From: Tom, COO
To: Leadership Group
Subject: FWD: Strat. Plan Decisions

Okay, guys, here he goes again, getting everybody and their brother involved. He's likely to backtrack on everything that took us weeks to decide. Who's got ideas on how to stop this train wreck before it gets out of the station? Anyone?

Tom

Sent: August 29, 2:30 p.m.
From: Ann Marie, CTO
To: Tom; Leadership Team
Subject: RE: FWD: Strat. Plan Decisions

Good call, Tom. You know he's going to get everyone's input and then change his mind a hundred times before we get going. I say we just ignore him and keep going, tell him that everyone loved the plan, and this is how it is. He'll be fine. It's how I get him to agree to sign off on any of the financial items. He just can't make a decision to save his life.

Ann Marie

Sent: August 29, 2:58 p.m.
From: Judy, CFO
To: Leadership Team
Subject: RE: RE: FWD: Strat. Plan Decisions

Guys, you know this is his process, so I'm not sure we should interfere. Let's just wait till he's done and then change what we need to. Unless any of you think otherwise? I'm completely open to doing this a different way.

Judy

Sent: September 24, 3:26 p.m.
From: Sarah
To: CEO; Leadership Team
Subject: Strat. Plan Assignments

Hi, Steve.

I'm having a little trouble assigning goals and tasks to people. Everyone wants to be on the IT initiative for the new building, but no one wants to work on the marketing or compensation initiatives, let alone the innovation strategy. Some of the assignments were pretty vague, so I couldn't really explain what they were, and about 40 people haven't even bothered to sign up for anything.

I'm not sure what you want me to do.

Sincerely,

Sarah

Sent: September 24, 3:34 p.m.
From: CEO
To: Sarah; Leadership Team
Subject: RE: Strat. Plan Assignments

Hi, Sarah.

Well, that is a pickle, isn't it? I'm sure we can figure it out. Why don't you put a meeting on the calendar for the leadership team, and we'll white board some ideas. Maybe at the end of the month, because I'm sure by then more people will have stepped up to the plate.

Steve

Sent: November 2, 12:02 p.m.
From: Sarah
To: CEO; Leadership Team
Subject: Strat. Plan Assignments

Hi, Steve.

I hate to bring this up again, but we're still waiting for about 25 people to sign up for tasks, and we still have multiple goals and tasks without anyone assigned to them. It seems like we've already missed some deadlines. I'm not sure this is the right approach, but I just did the seating chart for my sister's wedding, and we made a big chart with all the tables and cut out the names of everyone coming and started placing them around. Maybe we could use that approach?

I've never been able to get that meeting scheduled due to everyone's competing priorities, so let me know if you guys still want to white board it through.

Also, not sure what you want me to do with all the feedback and questions I've been forwarding to you. It's been a few months, and no one has responded to them.

Just let me know how to proceed.

Sincerely,

Sarah

Sent: November 15, 1:15 p.m.
From: Steve
To: Sara; Leadership Team
Subject: RE: Strat. Plan Assignments

Hi, Sarah.

Thank you so much for checking in on this. With the holidays and all, let's set up a meeting for January and get this thing put to bed. By then we should have enough opinions to finalize the execution strategy!

Steve

LET'S GET REAL

I think we all know where this execution plan is headed: to the crossroads of Nowhere and Purgatory. Indecision cripples strategic-plan execution more than anything else. Whatever enthusiasm you had going at the start will quickly fade from the lack of a timely decision from leadership. In our example above, not just the CEO but all of them seemed stuck in the same indecision Twilight Zone; all waiting for someone else to make the call.

You don't need to be right, but you do need to choose. Leaders who wait for consensus on everything doom the plan to paralysis. Nothing gets launched, and everyone goes back to business as usual. People figure out how to make the same stuff happen that they did yesterday, but NOT how to execute on a new plan. Waiting for all twelve members of the jury to agree will keep things stuck in yesterday's paradigm. Leading a successful execution strategy requires making decisions in a timely manner. Have a plan for people if they make a mistake, but empower them to keep moving forward—proper strategic execution requires it.

CHAPTER 15

THE PLAN IS THE PLAN IS THE PLAN

This is the story of George. George is an executive at a large manufacturing plant employing approximately 250 people. Throughout his career he's been called the golden boy or the one with the golden touch. Everything he's ever set out to do professionally has turned out exactly as he planned.

So, naturally, when it came time to expand the facility to accommodate the large part orders they anticipated, he went about it with the same rigor he applied to anything he did: plan, plan, and then plan some more. He was confident that his success was due to his meticulous planning efforts, and he was not about to change his methods now. After all, he had been rewarded handsomely for this all his life. In his mind, George knew he was GREAT, and life confirmed it for him every damn day.

He worked with his team to create an execution plan for the strategic initiative, which called for another building equal in size to the current building, and adjoined by a "work corridor." He envisioned beautiful offices lining the work corridor connecting the two plants, and they would be filled with all the plant managers and administrative staff—including a beautiful, big office for George that looked out over all he had created.

Once the plan was solid in his mind, he went about lining up the various resources to get it built, and the permits sailed through like clockwork, and construction began. Once again, George was on track for yet another win and another big, fat bonus! He could envision the Maserati he had ordered and the safari to Africa that he was going to take with his perfect wife and 2.4 children. Life was good for Golden Boy George!

Not long after construction began, rumors that the anticipated "big order" might not be as big as they all expected started to surface. The airline industry was starting to slow, and there were some regulatory issues with the winglets for that particular model of plane. The sales head brought the concern to George, but George dismissed it offhand, saying it was just a rumor, and forged ahead with the plan. He was certainly not going to let anyone or anything get in the way of his plan. This had been identified as a possible threat when they were doing their SWOT and was dismissed as implausible. Therefore, according to George, it would not happen.

The new plant had reached about 90 percent completion when the engineers discovered a potential problem with the connecting work corridor. They determined it might be subject to flooding due to a small creek running adjacent to the plant, which had a propensity to flood every hundred years or so.

Did George want to elevate that section of the building?

"Absolutely not," said George. The plan was in place, and it was *highly* unlikely they would have that level of threat—it was not in the plan. He was really getting irritated by all these interruptions to his plan. Why couldn't they just trust his golden instincts?

Within six months the plant was complete, resplendent in

its glory, and George was more than pleased with himself that the construction wrapped up on time, on budget, and—most importantly—on plan. He invited the board and local dignitaries for the ribbon cutting, and all was right with the world. George could not wait to pick up his new Maserati and had booked the safari. Life was good as long as you stuck to the plan!

Two days after the ribbon cutting, the airplane manufacturer put its standing order for winglets on hold. George was not worried; he had been through downturns before. His competitors would have difficulties, not George. He continued with hiring and production as if the order was unchanged, believing it would be just a delay, not a cancellation. This was in their plan, after all. Two weeks after the grand opening, the standing order was canceled. George was frozen. There was nothing golden about this. He had never had one of his plans go awry, and he was confused—*what was happening?* He had a plan, right?

George and the sales team tried to resurrect the order, but the airline had a clause that allowed them to cancel the order without consequences, so there was nothing they could do. George was furious the airline was not adhering to the plan—it was wrong of them!

To add to George's troubles, the rainy season had begun, and with twice the average annual rainfall! Some were predicting an infamous hundred-year flood. The engineers implored George to do something to protect the building, particularly the beloved work corridor. However, George was too distracted by the canceled order to pay attention to any of the warning flags the engineers were waving.

A week later, the nearby river, and consequently the creek George had been warned about, started to overflow its banks. Within a day the entire work corridor was two feet under water, and both plants were at risk of flooding as well. George was now in a full-scale panic—so much so that he was still sitting in his pristine new office in the work corridor with water up to his knees. His assistant called the plant managers to come and get him out, but he refused to move—frozen in fear because his "plan" had fallen apart.

He couldn't understand: it had been so perfect in his mind. *What was happening?*

They finally called 9-1-1. George had to be rescued and sent away to a rehab facility due to a mental breakdown. No safari, no Maserati, no bonus, a completely ruined plant, bankruptcy, and—most concerning to George—a failed plan.

LET'S GET REAL

Moral of the story? Be flexible to avoid the otherwise inevitable failure. The plan needs to bend when the circumstances that the plan was built on change.

Good old George did not have a flexible bone in his body and could not see how to do anything differently than he always had. Having never experienced failure, he ignored critical information that might have allowed him to alter his path. When certainty and ego are involved, crucial questions never get asked, let alone answered.

George may seem like a far-fetched caricature of an out-of-touch white-collar executive, but he's all too familiar. Mistakes happen, Mother Nature happens, accidents happen, people change their minds, and all can be dealt with as they happen. But only if the plan and the people involved are ready for the unexpected.

No plan is perfect, and a perfectly executed plan left unchanged in the face of new information is just as bad as having no plan at all—doomed to failure. Good leaders know how to be flexible and are always watching the horizon for those things that might have changed—consequently requiring a change in plans. It's not sacrilegious; it's good planning.

CHAPTER 16

S.M.A.R.T. GOALS ARE DUMB

A TALE OF TWO CEOS

John was a numbers guy—always enamored with how he could measure literally everything and everyone. He had statistics tracking how often people were late for work, and could predict when the next person would be late, based on his calculations. His office walls were covered with charts and graphs measuring everything, from *which* customers bought *what* and *when*—and the number of steps to process an order— to the average number of minutes associates took in a break. You get the picture: if it was trackable, it was being tracked by John.

John called it his SMART goal strategy on steroids. Specific, measurable, achievable, results-based, and time-bound—at least that's what it was supposed to mean, but John took it to mean that if it could be tracked or measured, it could be made SMART. Most people who worked for John thought he was a nutter and just a little obsessive. But since he never actually did anything with his charts and numbers except stare at them, he was viewed as relatively harmless.

He had heard about SMART goals as a way to track the execution of strategic plans, so he assumed it was good to apply to anything he wanted to look into. The rest of the executive team humored him, let him track his things, went on about their day-to-day business, and gave very little thought to the strategic plan. John had rendered it inert with his obsession with tracking noncritical, irrelevant items, which were not tied to the plan.

...

Jean is also a CEO, but her approach to the execution of the strategic plan is completely different than John's, who is, by the way, her twin brother. Both Jean and John got in the right line at birth and were born to very wealthy parents, both of whom had trust funds and a few family businesses. Each got to pick the one they wanted to run when they turned twenty-five.

Not to be outdone by her brother, Jean decided to embrace SMART goals too. She knew John was obsessive and that his staff made fun of him behind his back, so she was determined not to suffer the same humiliation. She prided herself on being much more self-aware than John. Jean gathered her team and told them that this year she was going to use SMART goals to track the execution of the strategic plan. She patiently explained what they were and told her team to get started on coming up with a few metrics for each goal.

She was really pleased when, two weeks later, they presented her with dates assigned to all the goals. Wow, this was great! She had successfully implemented SMART goals! In her mind, they didn't need to bother with all those silly charts that John used or even with how they would measure some of this stuff.

They had a goal and a deadline—what more did they need?

...

Both John and Jean bumbled along leading their respective companies, and at mid-year review time, the family board of advisors asked for each to present a summary of his or her progress on the aforementioned plans.

John didn't need input from his team; he had all the numbers anyone could want. He began putting them all into a spreadsheet presentation that would wow the board.

Jean decided to get an update from her team as to how things were going. She called a meeting, and everyone presented updates on their progress toward the SMART goals. Sadly, the goals that had deadlines in the past six months had not been achieved, and it wasn't looking good for the future dates either. When she asked what the problem was, she was given a variety of excuses—all of which sounded like "blah, blah, blah" to her. Somehow, she needed to make this presentable in a way that would show the board how good she was doing. *Aha!* She would have everyone revise the dates to sometime after the board meeting, and she would surprise them with all the progress. *Man,* did she love this SMART goal thing—it was brilliant.

The board meeting came, and five minutes into John's presentation, one of the board members stopped him and asked what the hell he was talking about, and how did these numbers relate to the execution of the plan? John fumbled, mumbled, and could not understand why they didn't love his approach to SMART goals as much as he did. Another board member simply asked what he had accomplished in the last six months related to the plan, and John just stared—*couldn't they see? Were they blind?* He was asked to sit down.

Then it was Jean's turn. Pleased with herself that she got to go after John's blunder, she would be a superstar. She presented her progress and outlined her SMART goals. One board member asked how the goals tied into the plan and why everything was due in the fourth quarter. Quick on her feet, Jean answered that these were *big* SMART goals, so they took time and they *were* the plan. *Geez,* she thought, *how dense are these guys?*

Then another board member said that her progress was no different than John's and that they needed to start holding their teams accountable and figure out a way to measure things appropriately so that the board can tell whether or not they were on track to achieving the goals of the plan—for which the board had paid a pretty penny to have developed.

Both Jean and John left the board meeting upset that they had not been feted in the way they were used to, and went back to doing things exactly as they had been. What did the board know about SMART goals anyway?

LET'S GET REAL

SMART goals are just a way of tracking goals, not a replacement for a good strategy. If you set the wrong goal, making it SMART will not make it right. As our hapless John did, many executives get caught up in the over-tracking of everything— somehow thinking this will get them closer to accomplishing something. No. That only creates confusion, frustration, and endless spreadsheets.

Jean didn't fare any better, thinking that having a deadline made her goals smart. She forgot to create a way to measure them. A date by itself is kind of meaningless if you don't know how you'll know if a goal was achieved by that date.

SMART goals are a way to track the progress of the

execution of your plan. They are not a substitute for good leadership. You have to have a good plan to start with, tracking the most important goals, in the right order, with the right metrics and achievable date targets. If you don't, it's just a spreadsheet that nobody cares about or dates that are meaningless because there are no consequences for missing the targets.

Good leaders hold people accountable to the plan. SMART goals are simply a tool for helping them to do so.

SECTION 3

EXIT RAMP DETOURS

Strategies that don't start with the end goal in mind will usually miss the exit ramp every time. Founders of small to midsize companies rarely think about the day they will sell or be forced out of the business. Unless, of course, they run a tech company funded by venture-backed capital that wants nothing more than to take an exit to line their pockets and flip to the next big thing. All the Silicon Valley wannabes will have gobs of support to make sure they take the right exit ramp at the right time—the rest of you will actually have to plan for it.

Founders are often caught flat-footed when the best offer of their life comes along. Like someone fitted with lead boots, they fail to act and the buyer goes sailing by like a cigarette boat in the Hamptons. Or they are so entranced with the sketchy investment banker who wants to fleece the company, they fail to see their company is being stolen right out from under them. Worse yet is the founder whose company has long outgrown his skill set and who is literally paralyzed with fear about what comes next. Well, if he stays in paralysis too long, it will be the wailing a life-support machine makes when someone pulls the plug.

Strategic offer, selling to friends, maybe even family? Who knows? "I'll know it when I see it"—the common response from the entrepreneur who has no idea what their business is even worth. The need for cash or a certain dollar amount has no real connection to the value of the business—not that they actually know what the value of the business is. As the saying goes, "If you don't know where you're going, any road will take you there." So goes the road toward an exit—hop on and pray the road is paved and the sign to the exit ramp is lined like the yellow brick road.

If any of this sounds familiar, you could be headed down the road to Nowhere when you decide to leave your business. Read the following eight noteworthy stories of how NOT to create a strategy for exiting your business, and maybe, just maybe, you'll pick up a few tips on how to do it right. Unless of course, you picture yourself like Cruella de Vil and absolutely have to have all one hundred puppies for yourself.

CHAPTER 17

LOST & FOUNDER

Sent: June 22, 2:00 p.m.
From: Jane, Director of Marketing
To: Bob, Director of Business Development
Subject: Craig's Role

Bob,

Have you seen Craig this week at all? I thought he was coming to the quarterly marketing meeting, but he was a no-show. Does he have a new schedule, or...?

Jane

Sent: June 22, 3:00 p.m.
From: Bob, Director of Business Development
To: Jane, Director of Marketing
CC: Ed, Director of Operations
Subject: RE: Craig's Role

Jane,

I think he went fishing on Monday. He put some pictures on the company Facebook page that I think he meant to put on his personal page.

Ed, do you know if he interviewed that candidate you have for supervisor? I saw the guy in the lobby; he looked lost.

Bob

Sent: June 22, 3:30 p.m.
From: Ed, Director of Operations
To: Jane, Director of Marketing; Bob, Director of Business Development
CC: Sue, Receptionist
Subject: RE: RE: Craig's Role

Bob and Jane,

Nope. He was a no-show. He said he wanted to interview all candidates for supervisory positions, but he missed the last one and was a no-show for this one. I need to make this hire, so I'm just going to do it without him.

Sue, do you know where Craig is?

Ed

Sent: June 22, 4:00 p.m.
From: Sue, Receptionist
To: Jane, Director of Marketing; Bob, Director of Business Development; Ed, Director of Operations
CC: Matthew, COO
Subject: RE: RE: RE: Craig's Role

All,

I do not know where Craig is, but I usually keep his calendar. I can tell you that the bank is coming in for a three-hour meeting tomorrow, so I assume he'll be here.

Matthew, are you in that meeting?

Sue

Sent: June 22, 4:30 p.m.
From: Matthew, COO
To: Jane, Director of Marketing; Bob, Director of Business Development; Ed, Director of Operations; Sue, Receptionist
CC: Jill, Director of HR
Subject: RE: RE: RE: RE: Craig's Role

All,

Craig has decided to take on a more limited role as CEO so that his schedule is more flexible. Please copy me on any important meetings you were expecting him to be in.

Matthew

Sent: June 22, 5:00 p.m.
From: Bob, Director of Business Development
To: Jane, Director of Marketing; Ed, Director of Operations; Sue, Receptionist; Matthew, COO
CC: Jill, Director of HR
Subject: RE: RE: RE: RE: RE: Craig's Role

Was he going to announce this to the management team, or are we just now finding this out? Who is approving my budget? Who's on point to close the new business that we just landed?

Bob

Sent: June 22, 5:30 p.m.
From: Jane, Director of Marketing
To: Bob, Director of Business Development; Jane, Director of Marketing; Ed, Director of Operations; Sue, Receptionist; Matthew, COO
CC: Jill, Director of HR
Subject: RE: RE: RE: RE: RE: RE: Craig's Role

I have a quarterly strategic-marketing plan that was due today. Who am I presenting to now?

Jane

Sent: June 22, 6:00 p.m.
From: Sue, Receptionist
To: Bob, Director of Business Development; Jane, Director of Marketing; Ed, Director of Operations; Sue, Receptionist; Matthew, COO
CC: Jill, Director of HR
Subject: RE: RE: RE: RE: RE: RE: RE: Craig's Role

He's supposed to tweet something about company strategy. It's in his calendar. Should I tweet something for him? What should it say?

Sue

LET'S GET REAL

And in a few short hours on a random Monday, Craig completely abdicated his position as CEO. *Congrats on your retirement, Craig!*

"Surround yourself with great people and let them do their jobs" is excellent advice for any leader or CEO. Never forget it and practice it every day. But it does not mean that as a CEO you can or should be an absentee leader, and it certainly does not mean the role of CEO isn't essential and needed. Many leaders—and this is especially true for company founders—lose sight of their job description and duties over time. They surround themselves with capable and talented people, and the actual job description of the CEO becomes muddled. These leaders often feel nonessential to the business, or they may feel that they are too tempted to meddle, so they dissociate themselves from the day-to-day operations.

Once their businesses grow to the point of having strong senior-management teams, many founders have reached their burnout point. They may have been at it for ten to twenty years, or perhaps the business has outgrown them and they no longer feel like they know enough about the business to add value. Whatever the case may be, take a break to rejuvenate if you must, but do not abdicate such an important role without being crystal clear with your team about who's really running the show.

If you are the CEO and intend to remain the CEO, you must do the job. Consider writing, or having someone else write, a renewed job description with specific duties and responsibilities. Are you doing this job? Do you want to do this job? Because if you don't, you can't have the title regardless of your ownership status.

If you're an owner, consider taking yourself off the org chart and promoting your number 2 person to president or CEO. If you are not an owner and are merely holding a title with no accountability, then you're doing the business a disservice.

Chief executive officer is the highest-ranking position in any business, and whoever has this title is accountable for all management decisions. This role means you show up and do the job, or you make the toughest management decision of them all, and you make it for yourself: you're not the right person for the job.

CHAPTER 18

GETTING SWEET ON SUGAR DADDY

Sent: December 12, 2:10 p.m.
From: Savannah, CEO
To: James, Partner, Private Equity Investments of North America
Subject: Dinner? Holiday cocktail?

Hi, James.

We met at a recent WPO conference. I hope you remember me. I am the founder and CEO of Pouty & Pretty Cosmetics.

I really enjoyed our conversation! You gave me such great advice about growing my business, and it left me energized and ambitious about the future. You have such amazing experience growing businesses like mine.

I was also really flattered that you think it has such potential. I'd love, love, love to meet up with you again sometime soon. Let me know if you're ever in town, or if I come out your way, I'll let you know. Either way, let's find a way to keep in touch.

All my very best,

Savannah

Sent: December 12, 3:22 p.m.
From: James, Partner, Private Equity Investments of North America
To: Savannah, CEO, Pouty & Pretty Cosmetics
Subject: RE: Dinner? Holiday cocktail?

Well, hello there. How nice to hear from you, Savannah. Of course I remember you. How could I not? I'd also love, love, love to get together and hear more about your business. Not only does your business have great potential, YOU have great potential.

Aligning with PPEI North America would be a very smart move for you. In fact, if I do say so myself, I could make you a rock star in the cosmetics industry.

Text me.

Jim

All right! You snagged one! Great job, Savannah. You've got your first big potential investor on the hook. Now all you have to do is work it, girl. Work. It. Jim's no dummy—he's been around the block a few times—and he knows the best way to get a smokin'-hot deal on a budding business is to flatter the daylights out of the unsuspecting founder and make her feel like she's the most brilliant woman in the world. Not only are you going to have a wealthy benefactor on your side, but you're also going to be hanging with the dealmakers, the "PE guys." As they say, now you're peeing in the grass with the big dogs.

So make your appointment now for a full spa day before you see Jim next, because he's your golden ticket. Pretty soon the cash will be flowing in and you'll be on a press blitz like no other, announcing to the world your big, new business deal. Look at you go!

Way to break the glass ceiling!

LET'S GET REAL

RANT ALERT!

We'd like to think a scenario like this is a thing of the past, but it's not. It's very real, and it happens every day. So this is our chance to speak directly to women like Savannah in the business world and say one thing: Show some self-respect and self-awareness, and *knock it off.*

Look, it's true: the big-money world is still a man's game. Look around the private-equity and banking world and tell us that's not true. It's true, and it's going to remain true until we get more women in positions of power—in government and in the private sector. Across the board we are still in the minority. Hell, we still have to work the equivalent of three additional months a year on average to even make equal pay to what most men are paid.

So, Savannah—and women like Savannah—why do you have to make it harder for the rest of us by believing that you have to charm your way into the big-money game? Or into any business game, for that matter? Most of us who have bought or sold businesses have been the only female in the boardroom before. It can be intimidating and throw you off your best game. But we are counting on you to step it up and show up with your strategic thinking and your personal power, not a demure-and-fawning-high-school-girl act.

Sound rough? It's meant to. But listen up, we're not done. Charming your way to the top, or into the big-money game, is only going to achieve one thing: getting taken to the cleaners— and it will be your fault.

If you show up with a flirty, forward attitude, you will have a giant sign over your head that says, "I got lucky and started this business, and I have no f$*#ing idea what I'm doing, so please flatter me and give me a 2x multiple and make me feel great about it!" Then you can go brag to your business friends and other female CEOs about how brilliant you are now that you are on the inside of the private-equity world.

Please.

CHAPTER 19

THE IMPOSSIBLE DIVORCE

Sent: November 2, 4:23 p.m.
From: Stan, CEO, Stan the Man Movers
To: Exec. Team Partners
Subject: Valuation & Offer

Guys,

The valuation came back today from Princeling Partners, and it looks exactly like what we've been hunting for: $25M plus shares in the new company. So we all benefit greatly. I think it's the right time to go ahead and get serious about this.

See the attached and let's discuss in our meeting on Friday.

STM (Stan the Man)

Sent: November 6, 2:00 p.m.
From: Stan, CEO, Stan the Man Movers
To: Exec. Team Partners
Subject: Meeting Outcome

Guys,

Well, that meeting didn't go as we planned, but let's all pull together and come to a consensus on this. I know some of you are afraid of selling, but let's talk about it. I gave you all shares in the business years ago so we could all benefit from an event like this—I really don't understand what the hesitation is.

Friday huddle to work it out. I'll go with the group, but let's be reasonable about this. I don't want to have to point out that I have 43 percent of all the shares!

Just kidding. Let's talk on Friday.

Sent: November 10, 12:10 p.m.
From: Stan, CEO, Stan the Man Movers
To: Exec. Team Partners
Subject: Decision

Guys,

I think we can all agree that that was a horrible meeting. However, we finally got a consensus that we'll move ahead with Princeling Partners to represent us in going to market. I'll get the formal engagement moving forward.

STM

Sent: November 10, 12:27 p.m.
From: Joanie, CFO
To: CEO; Exec. Team Partners
Subject: RE: Decision

STM,

I think I speak for everyone in saying that we were disappointed that you forced us to agree to sell. We are happy with the current company and the outcomes. It seems foolish to want to sell now, just when we're doing so well.

While we will forever be grateful for your generosity in giving us our original shares, we also want what's best for the business and all of its employees, which is why we agreed to explore options.

Joanie, CFO

Sent: November 22, 1:56 p.m.
From: Stan, CEO, Stan the Man Movers
To: Exec. Team Partners
Subject: Letter of Intent

Guys,

Really happy to share that we have a great first letter of intent from a terrific partner that I'm really excited about. As the point man for this, I'll keep you all informed. I've created a private shared drive for all the materials so you're all kept in the loop as partners. First step is the financial review, so Joanie will be instrumental in making this happen!

STM

Sent: November 23, 10:05 a.m.
From: Joanie, CFO
To: CEO; Exec. Team Partners
Subject: RE: Letter of Intent

Team,

Just a reminder: I'll be out over the Thanksgiving holiday, and since I have a ton of PTO that I haven't used, I'm going to go ahead and take off till the first of the year to use it up. You'll be fine with Sandy, our controller, although I wouldn't involve her in the sale stuff—you know how she can gossip!

Happy holidays, everyone!

Sent: November 23, 10:44 a.m.
From: Stan, CEO, Stan the Man Movers
To: Joanie, CFO
Subject: Vacation

Joanie,

Please come talk with me about this vacation you are taking. We need you as a part of the team to walk them through our financials.

STM

PHONE CALL TO PRINCELING PARTNERS:

STM: Hey, guys, Joanie is going to be out till the first of the year. Is there a way we can postpone the review?

Princeling: Nope. Did you know this?

STM: Well, she says she told me, but I sure don't remember it. Sandy, our controller, can do it, but she's likely to spill the beans. I guess I could do it, if that works? I know where most of it is.

Princeling: Well, that will have to work for now. I hope that nothing comes up that we don't know about.

Sent: December 16, 3:32 p.m.
From: Stan, CEO, Stan the Man Movers
To: Exec. Team Partners
Subject: Review Update

Guys,

We are only about a third of the way through the review as I'm winging it without Joanie. For whatever reason, a lot of the records we need are missing or misfiled. I guess she implemented a new filing system in November that no one understands.

The buyer is getting a little anxious about this, so I'm wondering if one of you could help me. I really want to project strength and competence among the partners, so who's in?

STM

Sent: December 17, 2:08 p.m.
From: Steven, CTO
To: CEO; Exec. Team
Subject: RE: Review Update

STM,

I know this is something you really want, Stan, but I have to say I'm still having doubts. Maybe Joanie being out is a sign that this isn't the right time. We can do what these buyers want us to do, so how about we pull it off the market and give it a go ourselves? I think I speak for the rest of the team when I say this.

Steven

Sent: December 17, 2:11 p.m.
From: Exec. Team
To: CEO; Exec. Team Partners
Subject: RE: RE: Review Update

Ditto—hey, we finally agree on something!

LET'S GET REAL

Trying to get two people to agree on something is difficult. Dealing with multiple partners can be excruciating. So begin with the end in mind. BEFORE you offer partnerships with active, voting shares to anyone in your company, spell out the rules of the road, such as who gets to make the big decisions about when and to whom to sell the business—let alone for how much.

If you're already in a partnership that is less than cordial, time to fix it before you decide to sell. Get a mediator, get a lawyer, or get anyone else to help the two of you duke it out about the rules of partnership. You might consider a shotgun clause: if you offer to buy out your partner for any amount and they say no, they can buy you out for the same amount. This prevents people from making frivolous offers.

Most business partnerships are entered into with about as much thought as going to the pound and picking out a dog. At least a dog is trainable and usually does what you say—a partner is another breed altogether. A business partnership is messy, and trying to sell with partnerships can become akin to the War of the Roses. Start the partnership with some simple rules in place, and the war will likely be more of a skirmish than the mother of all battles.

CHAPTER 20

LOYALTY TO COMRADES

Sent: September 1
From: Dean Chompers, CEO
To: Rick Dogood, Premium Investors
Subject: Offer Letter

Rick,

I have some serious concerns about the offer and the deal points.

In section 3, it discusses the payout packages for Larry and Joe, both of whom have been with me forever. I distinctly remember telling you that they needed to have positions in the new venture, not just a severance and buyout. What's going on here?

Chomp

Sent: September 1
From: Rick Dogood, Premium Investors
To: Dean Chompers, CEO
Subject: RE: Offer Letter

Chomp,

Not to worry, my man. I'm still working it for you. We'll get them some-thing, but like we've said, these guys are a little long in the tooth and might really benefit by us just throwing some money at them so you're not saddled with deadwood in the new venture.

These guys really want you and the staff that's under 50—can you see their point? Your buddies are way past their prime, and the last time they came up with anything innovative was WWII! Just kidding, but you get what I mean.

I know you're loyal to them, but won't money help ease the exit a bit? They can ride off in their golf carts and have enough to play every day and visit the new massage parlors next to Mar-a-Lago!

C'mon, let's get creative and see if we can come up with something that will make their eyes pop and their wallets bulge.

Rick

Sent: September 2
From: Dean Chompers, CEO
To: Rick Dogood, Premium Investors
Subject: RE: RE: Offer Letter

Rick,

This is a deal breaker for me, Rick. These guys have been with me from the beginning. We graduated together. I know they may not be the sharpest tacks in the pack anymore, but they helped get me here, and I'm not going to give up on them now. Can't we find someplace for them in the new org that will bring this strategy together and takes advantage of all they bring to the table? There has to be a way.

Let's get creative with titles—how about Chief Fun Officer? Larry does stand-up comedy on weekends. Every company needs a laugh now and then, don't they?

And Joe will literally do anything; he's always been that kind of guy, so how about Chief Cleanup Hitter or Shortstop—you know, the extra guy on the field? You know it's a great idea. Besides, the board and the rest of the company will not be happy about sacking their two mascots. They're my brothers-in-arms!

Chomp

Sent: September 4
From: Rick Dogood, Premium Investors
To: Dean Chompers, CEO
Subject: RE: RE: RE: Offer Letter

I'm working it for ya, man, but it's not looking good. The board of the new company is not liking this direction at all and is going to get cold feet if we can't move past this.

Remember, they have your competitor in their sights if you don't pull the trigger soon—they would rather have you guys, but they're also willing to walk. But you know I'm in it for you first—you're my client, and I'm here to make you happy and get you a killer deal!

The sale to this company lines up so perfectly with your strategic and exit plans. Your three-year deal is killer, and the buyout will be fantastic if you hit your numbers!

Besides, Larry and Joe will make millions on the stock if this does what we are projecting.

Let's be reasonable here: if those guys are as loyal as you say, they'll do anything for you, so why wouldn't they take the package? This is really a win all around. Let's set up a call and talk it through—you know I'm right. Together we can make this happen.

Believe me, we'll give them as soft a landing as possible, but making up dumb titles will just make you look bad to the investors. Let's get your board on the call too and get their opinion.

Rick

Sent: September 6
From: Dean Chompers, CEO
To: Rick Dogood, Premium Investors
Subject: RE: RE: RE: RE: Offer Letter

Rick,

I told you from the start, I'm not going to budge on this one. They are my foxhole buddies, and they're coming with me. And I want them to have their current titles, Head of Engineering and Chief Technology Officer. I don't need to talk to the board, and I don't want to talk to anyone else. It's my company and my decision.

My wife told me to let them stay, so now I know I'm doing the right thing—if you can't stay loyal to your friends, then who can you count on? So you just go tell those dirty, money-grubbing bastards that if they want me and my company, they have to take all of us or none of us.

Chomp

Sent: September 12
From: Rick Dogood, Premium Investors
To: Dean Chompers, CEO
Subject: RE: RE: RE: RE: RE: Offer Letter

Chomp,

I tried to call you multiple times to discuss this, but since I can't reach you, here's the final offer. $20M upfront, contracts for you and all execs except Larry and Joe, same buyout and share price and deal points as before. If you want to keep Larry and Joe, you can, but it comes out of your contract fee and they get no shares in the new company, only what they currently own. They cannot keep their current positions, so feel free to make up whatever titles you want.

You'll notice the offer is now $5M less, which is their estimation of how much drag the new company will have with your buddies on board, even in made-up positions.

They are done negotiating, so this is the final offer. You have 24 hours to decide.

Rick

In the end ...

Chomp dithered on the decision—his buddies or $5M+ in his pocket with much more down the road? Sell to the best strategic buyer he could imagine, or place a higher value on friendship and loyalty? The deadline passed, and the investors pulled the offer and went to his competitor, and that deal was closed in record time. Chomp and his Chompsters struggled with cash flow and technology while the new venture cleaned their clock.

The company closed two years later, after filing for Chapter 7 bankruptcy—not the ending he imagined after thirty years of building the company. But the band stayed together—Larry, Joe, and Chomp (aka, Mo). All of them are still living by Mar-a-Lago, but can't afford golf or massages.

LET'S GET REAL

Loyalty to comrades will act like an anchor dropped from a boat traveling at full speed. The envisioned strategy will never be fulfilled if you have people on board that have long outlived their usefulness—either because they didn't grow with the business or simply don't have the skills to move up the chain or learn new things.

All good things must come to an end. And when you employ friends and family, don't count on a buyer placing the same value on them as you do. In fact, it's likely to really drag your valuation down when it's clear the company has performed *in spite* of them being involved.

When working an exit strategy, think long and hard about who will really be of value to a potential buyer, and have those hard conversations with the rest early on. Money will help grease the exit, but you'll have more of it if you do the right thing and help them out before you have to carry them on your back.

CHAPTER 21

DIVISION OF MULTIPLES

$$10 \div 4 \times 0 = 0$$

MINUTES OF PHOENIX RISERS'
BOARD OF DIRECTORS MEETING
NOVEMBER 18

9:01: Discussion of sale begins. Strategic plan has been successful; revenue growth, gross margin, and profit margin all aligned and on track based on feedback from Shuster & Schuckster Investment House.

9:16: CFO discusses the desire to push the multiple discussion from a 1x revenue sales model to a multiple of net profit that he believes will work better for all involved. He wants a 10x on net profit, which was $4M last year and projected at $5M this year, for a $50M valuation.

9:22: CEO points out it's a moot point as revenue is $50M, so at 10x net it would be the same. And it's easier to grow revenue than profits. He's also concerned the industry standard would be far lower than 10x—more like 6x on net—which would result in a lower sale price. What's the point here?

9:25: CFO discloses that he can work the books to show a much higher net profit; therefore, he can tweak the valuation higher if we can get Shuster & Schuckster to go for it.

9:27: CMO asks CFO how he plans on doing that.

9:29: CFO says it's not hard and uses white board to map it out.

9:30: CTO asks if this accounting method is legal.

9:33: Controller points out that it's not within generally accepted accounting principles (GAAP).

9:37: CFO gets agitated and shows how he could potentially get us double the valuation by using this method. And shows how it's legal.

9:40: CEO asks about tax implications as it seems like they might be significant.

9:42: CFO says no, it would all wash out in the end.

9:45: Controller interjects and says by her calculations it could be very significant in light of the fact that they would be recognizing revenue differently and could be subject to back taxes.

9:47: CFO shuts her down, saying he's looked into it, and the likelihood of that happening is insignificant.

9:55: Vote is taken to give CFO authority to change accounting practice to increase the company's reported net profit from 10% avg. to 21% avg.

Ayes — 8

Nays — 1 (Controller)

MEETING WITH SHUSTER & SCHUCKSTER BANKERS
DECEMBER 12:

S&S: Wow, what's with the new financials? Seems like your net went through the roof!

CFO: Yes, we're taking advantage of a new accounting principle that allows us to restate our financials this way. We assume that this will allow us to increase our go-to-market price by almost twofold as we'll be able to take advantage of a ten-times-net model of valuation.

S&S: Well, that is a possibility. But, of course, there will have to be a deduction in the valuation due to the outstanding tax bill you have now accrued due to the new accounting method.

CEO: Wait, what? I thought you said we wouldn't have any additional tax liability if we went to this method?

CFO: We don't; you guys are incorrect. I checked it out with the IRS and the State Department of Revenue before I amended our filing, and we fall in a different tax bracket now. I've been taking a night course at MSU; all the other CFOs are doing this too.

S&S: Guys, I hate to break it to you, but you're going to pay more taxes and it really doesn't change the valuation. In fact, it might lower it since your tax liability just went up exponentially. Did you consult a tax specialist before you did this?

CEO: This is ridiculous. We did this with the intent of raising the valuation, not lowering it! This is just wrong; you guys need to go to work for us and make it right!

S&S: Unfortunately, this is not in our control. The value of the business is the value of the business, regardless of how you guys want to play with the books. You can't suddenly say that you're making twice as much as before and think it will boost the value. It's based on industry standards, your company history, the strategic value to the buyer, and your projections. I'm afraid you guys really screwed the pooch on this one. Might want to go back and see if you can reverse the accounting methods, because we can't represent you at this stage—it looks like you're cooking the books! Sorry, guys.

CEO: Go f*&# yourself! This is a f*@&ing disaster!

LET'S GET REAL

Buyers are smart—the value is the value is the value. The only way to increase it is to increase your revenue and profits simultaneously and find the strategic buyer that will benefit the most from buying you. No one will pay for cooked books or suspect accounting methods in search of a higher multiple, regardless of whether it's a revenue model or a net-profit model.

If part of your strategic plan is to sell, research multiples from your industry and have a valuation done every few years, using various methods, to know in advance what a sale might net you. Waiting until you have a buyer or decide to sell is usually not when you should start doing your homework. You'd be taking the final for a class you have not attended.

Get smart and get prepared. Know what your company is worth, and know what you can do to improve the valuation—that's what you want to address in a strategic plan. Be like a Scout: always be prepared when you do decide to sell.

CHAPTER 22

THE PHANTOM OF THE OFFER

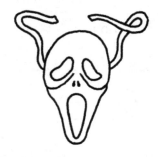

CEO Notes

Journal Entry

December 13

It's finally going to happen!!! I spoke to the broker today, and he confirmed the buyer is very interested and that we're in the ballpark of our asking price and the terms of the deal are all good. Boy, I never thought that this day would come; can't wait to do the happy dance and tell everyone that we made it across the finish line!

I'm so ready to be done with this place. Twenty years of growing it, managing all the people, problems, money, and strategies—I need to get out. I'll negotiate for a very short stint at the new place. Time to trade in the wife and find some new clubs! That reminds me, I had better start that process now so she doesn't get her grubby little hands on my pot of gold.

List of to-dos:

- Meet with financial planner to discuss what to do with my $20M

- Set appt. to go see property in NM

- Put deposit on sailboat—make final decision on extras

- Start divorce proceedings

CEO Notes
Journal Entry
December 26

I went ahead and shared the news with the executive team—there were mixed reactions. Several were concerned about their jobs—and their shares. I assured them that both would be taken care of. I could see the relief around the table, but I was surprised they weren't happier about the deal. Geez, this is what we have been working for! The CFO knew ahead of time, but even he was piling on with the Debbie Downers. I guess we should have said this is what we were working toward eventually. Who knows?

I cautioned them to keep it confidential, as the broker had told me to do. He said it could cause the deal to go south if word got out.

Met with the financial planner and the divorce lawyer. I'll be serving the papers on Tubby shortly. My financial guy said I should hold off on the property and the boat until the deal closes, just to be sure, but I'm a gambler so went ahead and did both. I'm ready to go—the finish line is so close I can see it!

CEO Notes
Journal Entry
January 15

I thought we would be further along by now, but, Jesus, this is really dragging out. The financial review is taking forever, and my CFO is completely consumed by it. All the books are on the up-and-up, so I don't get what the big deal is.

As expected, Tubby didn't take being served with divorce papers well. She went ahead and hired this hotshot lawyer and thinks I'm going to be paying his fees—think again, honey. That's on you!!

Apparently, someone leaked news about the sale, so a few more employees know something about it and have given notice. Really chafes my hide after all I've done for these guys. Can't they hang on and make the company look good till we cross the finish line? So far, though, the executive team is holding strong.

We also got notice from the landlord that they are jacking up the rent significantly next year, but we'll be out of here with the sale, so I'll just wait them out. Greedy bastards.

CEO Notes
Journal Entry
February 10

Christ, I can't believe this thing hasn't closed yet. The financial review is done, and apparently they want to revise the offer based on what they found—doesn't make sense to me, but I'll see what they have to say.

My nuts are really in a vice with "she who shall not be named." She booted me out of my own house, so I'm living in a goddamn hotel. I can't believe the law lets you do that—I've paid all these years for that place!! She should have to move out. I have to be careful what I say because I guess her shitbag attorney will be getting depositions from my employees about where I've been, what I've been doing, and where I might have hidden some money. Jesus. What a nightmare.

My sales VP gave her notice last week. That's a real blow to the gut. She's the best sales lead we've ever had, and her team is amazing. I offered her more money, but she said she didn't like the folks we'll be acquired by and has had many offers over the years, so she wanted to move on. I expect she'll probably have a few more follow her out the door, but it doesn't matter. We'll be part of a global team, so some of them would have gotten sacked anyway.

CEO Notes
Journal Entry
February 13

We got the new offer today, and it's not just a trim, it's a freakin' buzz cut. I can't believe the broker let this happen. I told him no way in hell would I agree to that. He also said that I have to tell them that the sales VP left, which apparently meant a lot to them—they wanted her as part of the deal. This is quickly becoming a nightmare. I sent the broker back with a modest reduction.

CEO Notes
Journal Entry
February 29

Thank God Leap Year only happens every four years, because this day has literally been the worst of my life. The buyers pulled out completely—said that the financials didn't support the price and that without my sales VP the revenue growth projections look shaky. Plus, they were spooked by the fact that we'd have to move since our lease is up and there are no options other than the ridiculous price the landlord offered.

They were also saying that my divorce proceedings make me a high risk, and they would require that to be finished before any deal could be done, because they don't want her to be a part of it. And that's just getting worse by the day. My kids aren't speaking to me, the Hampton Inn is a fleabag, and my CFO just quit without giving any notice at all.

When I brought in an outside CFO, I found out that he'd been stealing from me for a while, which is why the buyers went away. They figured it out before I did.

I lost the deposits on the NM property and my sailboat. I asked Tubby to take me back, but she's already dating, losing weight, and said she's much better off without my snoring, old, sorry ass beside her!

LET'S GET REAL

The deal ain't done till it's done and the money is in the bank. Anytime someone starts spending dollars they don't have, no good will follow. The first rule of preparing for a sale is to act as if it's not happening. You MUST run your business as if you will be there tomorrow, next month, and next year—not only to protect your investment in the business, but also to keep from falling so in love with the deal that you end up hating your business when it's over.

Deals fall apart every day—more often than they come together. They require confidentiality, patience, and above all else, a steely resolve to get through it knowing that if it doesn't work out, you have a terrific business to fall back on.

Don't spend money you don't have, don't tell people who don't absolutely need to know, carry on business as if nothing has changed, and don't do anything stupid to screw it up—like start a divorce proceeding. Investors and buyers want stability, and so do employees, so you have to walk the tightrope between the two. It ain't over till the fat lady sings, as they say.

CHAPTER 23

IDENTITY THEFT

Sent: October 18, 11:29pm
From: Jodi, Founder & CEO
To: Jen
Subject: Margaritaville!

Jen,

I'm so glad you talked me into taking this trip! I'm so excited!Just imagine—three weeks in sunny Mexico . . .I don't think I've ever taken a vacation for this long. Of course, I'll bring my laptop, tablet, and cell phone. Things are smoking hot in sales right now, and I've got to be on call morning, noon, and night. I also need to find a printer and fax machine for check signing and some important contracts that are coming up for renewal.

Sent: October 19, 8:30am
From: Jen
To: Jodi, Founder & CEO
Subject: RE: Margaritaville!

I thought you hired a VP of Sales last year . . . can't he handle it? And don't you have a CFO now that can sign contracts?

Sent: October 19, 8:34am
From: Jodi, Founder & CEO
To: Jen
Subject: RE: RE: Margaritaville!

Oh no. I approve all of the important strategic sales like I always have. Our new CFO has check signing authority, but I sign the checks. I don't always know what they are for, but I sign them just so it's my signature on them. *I'm the check signer.* I also need to be available to answer questions.

Sent: October 19, 8:42am
From: Jen
To: Jodi, Founder & CEO
Subject: RE: RE: RE: Margaritaville!

I thought you rounded out your executive management team with top talent. What questions would come up that couldn't wait? Can't they answer the day-to-day questions? We have all kinds of outings and activities planned. Are you going to be glued to your cell phone the entire time?

Sent: October 19, 8:40pm
From: Jodi, Founder & CEO
To: Jen
Subject: RE: RE: RE: Margaritaville!

I'm the CEO. Of course I'm going to be glued to my cell phone. It's my company. I need to know everything that is going on. Always. I mean, I have to know, to be informed, in case I need to make a decision. I didn't hire these people to make decisions on my behalf, I still need to make important decisions every day. Jim is doing a great job since I promoted him to president; mind you though, he's not the CEO. I'm the CEO. *I'm the decider.*

Sent: October 19, 8:46am
From: Jen
To: Jodi, Founder & CEO
Subject: RE: RE: RE: RE: Margaritaville!

Okay. Well . . . I guess, if you must. Seems like it kind of defeats the purpose of having that highly paid executive team and a president when you don't let them make any decisions. But at least you won't be glued to social media all day like you usually are.

Sent: October 19, 8:50pm
From: Jodi, Founder & CEO
To: Jen
Subject: RE: RE: RE: RE: Margaritaville!

Right . . . well, I'll have to tweet and post at least four times a day. We hired a social media vendor and they do a pretty good job staying on top of it, but I have to post myself. I have to do it. I'm the only one that can do it the right way. It has to be me. After all, *I'm the voice of the company.*

Sent: October 19, 8:50am
From: Jen
To: Jodi, Founder & CEO
Subject: RE: RE: RE: RE: RE: Margaritaville!

Okay, but are you sure you can't go offline for even a few days? I mean, what's the worst that can happen with such a capable team?

Sent: October 19, 8:52pm
From: Jodi, Founder & CEO
To: Jen
Subject: RE: RE: RE: RE: RE: Margaritaville!

I'm telling you, listen . . . the place would burn straight down to the ground without me. To. The. Ground. Now, let's have another margarita.

LET'S GET REAL

Okay, time for some tough love. If you built a successful company, there is going to come a time when you need the company much more than it needs you. If you were fortunate enough to acquire top senior talent and to have a steady and sustainable stream of revenue, and if that revenue is providing you with the means to explore other things that are fulfilling, then do so, guilt free.

Many business founders fail to recognize when they are no longer needed for the day-to-day operations of their business. Like Sue, they convince themselves that they are desperately needed and depended upon by their staff, when in truth, they have become the meddling founder who not only isn't needed, but ultimately, isn't wanted. The energy that your business needed to get off the ground may not be the same kind of energy that it needs when it has matured. And if you are unable to evolve your own identity, much as your business has evolved, it will forever be in service to you and your need to maintain that identity rather than to its employees, customers, and industry.

When founders recognize that they too need to evolve—that they too can grow and mature—so too can their businesses. Living co-dependently with your business is often times a requirement of a successful start-up: it's what you know, who you are, and how you've operated . . . it *is* part of your identity. But that notion doesn't mean you are a persona non grata without it. When your business matures to the point where it can operate without your attentiveness to every detail, recognize that milestone and revel in it! It's part of the reward of entrepreneurship and yours for the taking. It's the time at which you get to focus on your *personal strategy*: who you are, what you want, what makes you happy, and what plans you will lay out for the next chapters of your life.

Your team knows when you're not adding value and when you are staying connected simply because you think you're supposed to or you don't know what else to do. So get off the deck and climb to the top of the mast. See what lies ahead for your business and what lies ahead for you. It's the most valuable thing you can do for both parties.

CHAPTER 24

GRUBBING IT OUT

Congratulations, founder! You made it! The final chapter in your leadership journey has finally arrived. You have graduated from the school of hard knocks, clawed your way to the top, maybe even broken the glass ceiling, and the day is finally—*finally*—here.

After countless meeting with brokers, bankers, venture capitalists, private-equity guys, accountants, auditors, and every other white-shirt-and-blue-tie guy in town, you finally have a deal to sell your baby. Your one-and-only business, started from scratch with a credit card and a few good friends. Here you are, with a deal for enough money to live the rest of your life without ever having to stress about money, employees, customers, technology, email, or even getting up in the morning if you don't want to. You can do whatever you want, go wherever you want, for as long as you want, and never have to answer to anyone again.

Due diligence was a nightmare. Six long months of finance people digging through every bit of clean, moderately clean, and downright dirty piece of laundry you've got. They grilled you about your employees, scrubbed through your client contracts, analyzed every entry in your books, and forced you to rebuild your last three years of financials to their specifications. They dragged you all over the country to meet with other founders of businesses in their "roll-up strategy" and they've put you on display to board after board. They nearly broke you, but you knew it was worth it. You knew the payday was coming.

And here it is. Here's the term sheet. Go ahead, sign it. Make it happen. The future is right there on your desk...

But wait. It wasn't that bad. Maybe you could go through it again with a different buyer and get a BETTER deal! Maybe you could make enough money to live two or three lifetimes! Maybe you could double down for a few more years, make twice as much as this deal, and you'd be running with a whole different crowd, the big-money crowd. *Oh, the temptation!*

Your advisors say that your competition is on your heels and there's a downturn in the market coming. The dealmakers say that "money is moving right now," but predict a slowdown. *Phffff!* They're probably just saying that so you'll sign on the dotted line. If you can get a deal this big, why can't you get a bigger one? Look at you! You can do anything! And there's power in saying no, right? Turning down this offer will just make the other, bigger buyers want you even more.

Let's face it: it's simply not enough money.

LET'S GET REAL

All right, poker players, if you want to go all-in with your last hand at the end of the night when you've been on a roll and sitting at the table for twelve hours, then you just go right ahead. But that's not how we think great leaders should play the game.

There's something fundamental missing from our CEO's self-talk above: the consideration for what becomes of the business, the employees, and the customers after the deal is done. Money isn't the only currency changing hands when a business is bought or sold. There are people involved at every level, people who will likely remain with the business long after you're gone. So whether or not a "deal" is good for them should be an essential part of your decision-making.

There is also the legacy of your brand to consider—how you want it to be regarded and what you want it to be known for once it has changed hands. The brand itself may go away or be transformed into something new, but the story of what your business once was will always be there. How do you want that story to live on?

On the topic of actual currency: our CEO in the story above seems to be experiencing a self-inflicted doom loop. The doom loop occurs when you make more money than the people to your left but not as much as the people to your right, so you keep needing to make more money than the people to your right, then people next to *them*, and so on and so on. It's a never-ending doom loop when you are playing the game of one-upmanship.

We could go on for chapters about our respective philosophies about money, the kind of relationship we believe business owners should have with money, and our personal opinions about the social responsibilities we think people with money should have. But suffice it to say, if you are in the most fortunate position of being able to sell your business—by choice, not by necessity—then we think you should think first and foremost about these three things:

1. Are you being offered what your business is truly worth on the market? Not what it is worth to you, not what you want to be paid back for all those years of

barely making it, not what someone owes you for your pain and suffering of building a business, but what it is actually worth without you.

2. Will your employees and customers be treated respectfully? Will others who have invested their time and talent into the success of the business be given a soft landing after an ownership transition?

3. Are you clear there is nothing about your decision that is coming from a place of greed?

If you can answer yes to these three questions and there is a deal on your desk, then the time is now.

Congratulations, you made it! Now sit back, relax, and enjoy the legacy you're leaving. Give yourself a nice long break and don't do anything for a while. You've earned it.

But when you do decide to get back in the game, be sure to pass on what you've learned as a business leader. It's on all of us to make better leaders and better businesses for the future.

ABOUT THE AUTHORS

Mary Marshall's passion is helping entrepreneurs and executives achieve their dreams. Mary has been a CEO, an owner, and chief cook and bottle washer. She's been a Vistage Chair (member and executive) and has coached leaders to find their own success. In 2014, she published her first book, *Putting Together the Entrepreneurial Puzzle: The Ten Pieces Every Business Needs to Succeed* as a collection of answers to the most common problems that hamper small business success. Marshall Advisors, LLC is Mary's consulting practice in Seattle, which focuses on strategic planning, CEO and executive coaching, and leadership development. Mary speaks on Intentional Culture for organizations nationally. Since 2012, she has been active teaching a course for the Small Business Administration called "Emerging Leaders" that takes entrepreneurs through a seven-month course to create a strategic growth plan for their businesses. The course is considered a mini MBA.

Kim Obbink is an Art Center College of Design graduate who began her career as a graphic designer and over the years became an accomplished brand strategist and leader. She worked as both employee and vendor for many worldclass technology and entertainment companies, and ultimately served as CEO of a Seattle based digital marketing and talent acquisition company. Her experience brings high-altitude vision and strong brand strategy to everything she does. Kim believes that an authentic brand requires authentic leadership. Her vision that values and a well-stated, well-actioned belief system are the religion of every healthy organization is what she brings to her consulting work with growth-oriented companies today. An entrepreneur, strategist, writer, and artist, Kim has a colorful view of the world. That combined with a bold sense of humor allow her to share her unique perspective on how others can find success and satisfaction in being great leaders from the heart.

CPSIA information can be obtained
at www.ICGtesting.com
Printed in the USA
LVHW021446191020
669148LV00004B/201